PINK SLIPS and PARTING GIFTS
A novel

By

Deb Hosey White

Pink Slips and Parting Gifts

By
Deb Hosey White

All Rights Reserved © 2012 by White & Associates
ISBN: 978-0-9829179-2-3

For more information about this book, visit our website:
www.PinkSlipsAndPartingGifts.com

Cover image by Taylor Teodosio

For David

and

For the generations of
American retirees and workers who have
unfairly lost employer-sponsored health care benefits

It was a merger in name alone.

Introduction

WE LIVE IN AN AGE OF BUSINESS MERGERS AND ACQUISITIONS.

In 1934, the game of Monopoly made its first appearance in U.S. stores. Based on the wheeling and dealing of big business, Monopoly captured the essence of American commerce and capitalism. Within eighteen months it was the most popular game in the country with over 2 million copies sold to a nation struggling to emerge from the Great Depression. Since its introduction, an estimated 500 million people around the world have collectively spent billions of hours playing this game. Did all those hours of buying and selling prime real estate, collecting rents, passing GO, going bankrupt, borrowing from the bank and going to jail actually influence the American business psyche? We may never know for certain, but clearly somewhere along the way the Monopoly mentality was born.

Once upon a time the merger of two major U.S. corporations could prompt shockwaves in the business community and trigger lengthy court cases. But times change. In the infancy of the twenty-first century, mergers and acquisitions are commonplace.

Being one of the little people in a merger-acquisition should be a once-in-a-lifetime experience, but that's hardly true. Many mid-career workers have already survived several acquisitions. Some were hired by the right employer at the wrong time on multiple occasions; others have remained at the same desks as bigger and bigger conglomerates swallowed up their employers.

Mergers and acquisitions are messy business and they change the lives of everyday people. Everyday people, however, don't headline the business news. The newsmakers are those individuals lucky enough to be among the merger's change in control group. These are the power players on the seller's side of the negotiation table – senior executives who are likely to walk away

1

from the mess they've just made with cash and benefits beyond their wildest childhood dreams. For some, getting to walk away is almost as valuable as the cash.

Only the employees left behind to be assimilated understand the true meaning of a merger. In the initial years, post-merger organizations are never happy places, rarely productive places, and often very difficult places to work. The new employer generally views acquired employees as rogue players, testy and uncooperative; while the acquired employees often feel like outsiders, underappreciated and abandoned.

In the analysis of a merger, the official merger date is clearly determined. The origins of a merger, however, are more difficult to discern. Assuming the CEO doesn't hold controlling interest in the company, there are others who must be convinced that it's the right time to sell: major stockholders, the board of directors, the founder's widow.

When is the first time the CEO dares to say out loud, "It's time to sell the company"? Does he practice first in front of a mirror? Does he quietly float the idea to his most trusted colleague over a weeknight dinner? Does he first seek legal counsel? SEC guidance? Financial advice? Or possibly he moves straight to crafting a convincing report to the board of directors. If the CEO is gutsy enough, "selling the company" might quietly pass his lips for the first time during a clandestine meeting with the CEO of a potential buyer – setting the bait for a bid that will electrify the decision-makers back home.

Once a company is sold, most people only see the news headline, hear the sound bite, or watch the ninety-second report on TV network news. Those affected most directly by the sale of a company include shareholders, executives, employees and their families, competitors, communities, and retirees. The impact can be so significant to these groups that the facts of the sale are only part of the story. Speculation, opinion, and half-true tales are weighed and considered as details of the deal unfold.

As two companies merge, so many personal stories transpire that it would take a character like The Stage Manager in Thornton Wilder's *Our Town* to know all the parts. *Pink Slips and Parting Gifts* is the story of one merger that changed the lives of thousands of people in three short months. It is a peek behind the curtain at the events and emotions affecting a handful of these individuals – the joys, the pains, the absurdities, the excesses, the disbelief, and the rejection. Most of all, this is the story about fortunes made and lives disrupted. Remember that phrase the next time you hear a company has been sold. It replays itself every time another corporation changes hands and disappears from the big board on Wall Street.

PART ONE

ANNOUNCEMENT DAY

The End

"Mike! Stay awake!" In the back seat of the black luxury sedan, Jeffrey W. Elkins gripped his briefcase with his left hand and the edge of the seat with his right. The driver's head snapped up swiftly as he realigned the drifting car within the lines on the pavement. Elkins looked at his watch: 2:55 a.m. An hour outside Manhattan and at least three more hours to Washington. He planned to grab a quick shower, shave, change clothes, and then break the news to key employees before the 7 a.m. press release from the merger law firm in New York.

"So how old are your kids now?" Elkins asked the driver. Anything to keep this guy from falling asleep at the wheel, Jeffrey thought. As Mike began to answer, Elkins refocused on his own concerns. Good Lord, he contemplated, I've just inked a $13 billion deal to sell my company and I may not live to make it back to the office.

Elkins released his grip on the briefcase containing a set of documents that proved he was about to become one of the richest men in commercial real estate. Both sides had spent the past sixteen hours working out the financials of this historic agreement. Elkins was exhausted and had planned to sleep for a few hours on the way back to D.C. Instead he was engaging the driver in conversation to keep him from smashing into the Jersey barriers. Having just become a member of the platinum parachute club, it would be a sick joke indeed to die heading home on the New Jersey Turnpike without ever enjoying a penny of his new wealth.

Mike let off the gas. The car's deceleration made Elkins look out the window.

"Bad news Mr. Elkins. Looks like there's overnight road construction on the Turnpike tonight. Only one lane on this side for the next forty miles."

"Shit," Jeffrey seethed. First a drowsy driver, now construction delays. At this rate it looked unlikely he would make it back to the office before news of the merger reached the press. The deal had been held closely and moved quickly. Both companies managed to keep the circle of key players very small and very quiet. There were high-level executives as well as long-service employees who were about to get blindsided by this news, including Jeffrey Elkins' communications staff.

Elkins snapped open his cell and tapped the home number for his communications director. Three swift beeps sounded and Elkins looked at the Low Battery message on the small screen. Then the phone shut off.

"Mike, do you have a cell phone?"

"Sure Mr. Elkins, it's right here on the dash. But right now there's no signal where we are. This is always a bad area to get service. I'll let you know just as soon as we're back in range."

Elkins felt triumphant just hours ago as he left the Manhattan law firm and slid into the back of this sedan. The adrenaline rush hadn't lasted long. He was starting to feel a bit cheated. Why hadn't he stayed in New York with the attorneys for a celebratory drink? Certainly the announcement could have waited one more day. Yet he was the one who had pushed to move fast to assure no advance leaks to the press. Elkins was pragmatic – a financial guy to the bone with a degree from the Wharton School and a reputation for being a savvy negotiator. It was his wife who was the touchy-feely type, not him. Still, he began to wonder if the mild queasiness in his stomach together with this series of Turnpike dilemmas was some kind of a sign. Merciful heavens, Jeffrey thought. I must be exhausted to be thinking like this.

The traffic slowed to a crawl as it funneled through the flashing yellow lights and orange plastic barrels. Elkins rested his hand on the handle of his briefcase. Bright work lights washed over the road crew wielding jackhammers and road patch equipment. It was a steamy August night outside the comfortable temperature-controlled sedan but the noise and the smell of tar managed to penetrate the car. As the traffic rolled slowly, he watched the men with their rakes, shovels and smeared faces sweating in the night heat under the glaring lights. For a fleeting moment Jeffrey Elkins had the visual impression he was entering Hell.

The Beginning

Kate Cooper hit the snooze button again just as the phone on the nightstand rang. Her husband Matt had left for work fifteen minutes earlier, and now he was calling from the car – something he rarely did unless it was urgent. No good morning greeting, no hello. Matt was yelling.

"Those bastards! I can't believe they sold the company! I can't believe they sold the company and didn't even tell the employees!"

Kate sat up fast. "Where did you hear...?" Before she could finish her question, Matt was answering, still yelling, still angry.

"On the radio. They just announced on WTOP that Pratt-Miles is buying The Easton Company for $13 billion! Those f…"

Kate cut Matt off. "Calm down Matt. I know you're upset. So am I." She wanted to say, this is my employer who's selling out, but she knew better. The Easton Company had been a fixture in the community for nearly forty years. Hell, they'd built the community, and it wasn't only her husband who would be upset about this sale. Residents, local politicians, area businesses, and nonprofit organizations would all be impacted. Beyond her own situation, Kate thought about her fellow employees. The shock was sure to be far-reaching, and as human resources director, her phone would be ringing nonstop.

"Look, I need to get to work and find out what's going on. I promise I'll call you later. Thanks for letting me know. I'm glad I got the news from you."

Because she enjoyed her privacy, Kate really disliked cell phones. Although she thought they were great emergency devices, she hated the tether they provided at all hours, blurring the remains of any division between work and private time. Kate never left her cell phone on overnight, but if she had, she would have gotten the news from her division VP who had phoned and left a message at 6 a.m. There were only a half dozen executives in the deal's inner circle, and her boss had been one of them. But before Kate got to that message, her home phone rang again – almost as soon as she'd hung up with Matt.

"Yes?" Kate answered pointedly, anticipating Matt calling back with some follow-up thoughts. It was barely 7:30 in the morning and she couldn't imagine who else would be calling on her home phone at that hour, even with this early morning breaking news. The distinct gravely voice on the other end of the line delivered what would be the most memorable pronouncement of Kate's day.

"Good morning, Kate. I'm calling to offer you my condolences, and a job." Kate had known Ross Winston for nearly twenty years. A longtime business friend and a Washington insider, he always kept up with Kate's career. His greeting made Kate chuckle.

"Thanks Ross. You're a prince among men."

"Make me King. I'm certainly old enough to be King. So what the hell's going on over there? How the heck did this happen?"

"I'm about to go in and find out, Ross. I sensed something was up the past few days. I even wondered if we might be selling, but the reality of that idea seemed so far-fetched. Can I call you later?"

"What about my job offer?"

"Let me get back to you on that. I consider it the highest compliment."

"OK, but remember my offer came first – I may not be the highest bidder, but promise you'll remember I was first."

"I promise, Ross. Bye."

Kate headed for the bathroom and stepped into the shower before the phone could catch her again. The water pulsing on her tense shoulders did nothing to relieve the unreal feeling of literally waking up to the fact that the company was being sold and her corporate job was doomed. There would be no need for the services of two corporate offices. Feelings of excitement to learn the details of the deal mixed with her apprehension over the uncertainty and anxiety to come. Kate's stomach lurched and there was a rushing noise in her ears.

"One thing at a time," she exhaled as she dried her hair and dressed. Her short commute to work through the suburban landscape Easton had built would not give her time to ponder all the what-happens-next? scenarios. The phone rang again but Kate ignored it and the caller did not leave a message.

SEC Information

UNITED STATES SECURITIES AND EXCHANGE COMMISSION
WASHINGTON, D.C.
SCHEDULE 14A INFORMATION

Following is an email communication dated August 14 from Jeffrey W. Elkins, Chief Executive Officer of The Easton Company, to all Easton employees regarding the company's merger with Pratt-Miles Inc.

FROM: Elkins, Jeffrey
SENT: August 14 8:22 AM
TO: All Easton Employees
SUBJECT: Announcement
IMPORTANCE: High

I have some important news to convey to you about the future of The Easton Company. Earlier today, we agreed to merge our operations with those of Pratt-Miles Inc. Our board of directors and the board of Pratt-Miles have approved the transaction. Below is the press release that was issued at 7 a.m. this morning.

We know you will have many questions about this development. Next week you will be meeting with your department heads and division managers where you will be informed about the details of the agreement, how it will change the company and how it may affect our employees. After these meetings, if you have additional questions we encourage you to contact Human Resources. We are committed to a continued open dialogue with you concerning this process and will further update you as we move forward in completing the merger.

PRESS RELEASE
Dow Jones & Company, Inc.   August 14 (BUSINESS WIRE)

Pratt-Miles Inc. (NYSE: PMI) today announced the execution of a definitive merger agreement with The Easton Company (TEC). Under the terms of the agreement, which has been approved by each company's board of directors, shareholders of The Easton Company will receive $65 per share in cash. The total consideration will be approximately $13.4 billion including the assumption of approximately $3.8 billion of existing debt. The transaction is expected to close in the fourth quarter, and is subject to the approval of Easton shareholders, as well as customary closing conditions.

NOTE: This document includes forward-looking statements, which reflect our current view with respect to future events and financial performance. These forward-looking statements are subject to certain risks and uncertainties, which could cause actual results to differ materially from historical or anticipated results. The words "will," "plan," "believe," "expect," "anticipate," "should," "target," "intend" and similar expressions identify forward-looking statements. Readers are cautioned not to place undue reliance on these forward-looking statements.

For Easton employees, it was the first time the disclaimer in a company press release seemed more poignant than the content. Somewhere between leaving work the day before and opening this email from Jeffrey Elkins the following morning, a serious development had occurred. Each individual's anticipated plans, beliefs, expectations, and intentions regarding the future of their employment had fallen away.

On the Couch

What is it that makes a CEO decide to sell a company? What exactly goes into the mental process? What event sparks that first thought? What turns the thought into a consideration, a possibility? What makes him take the first step toward the final action – the signature on the deal?

Ah, to be a fly on the wall when the CEO spills his guts to his psychologist. To discover the truth behind the sound bite: "It wasn't any one thing, but a set of circumstances that made us sell."

Is it greed? Just too much money to be made to leave the fruit on the tree any longer.

Is it ego? Can't stomach the idea of someone taking your place at the top.

Is it jealously? Everyone likes your handpicked heir apparent better than you.

Fear? Succession planning gone awry – the next in line has newly discovered flaws and there's no alternative replacement in sight.

Financial worry? Concern that the competition is getting stronger, so better to sell out than be taken over.

Is it boredom? After a twenty-five-year career, rising from division head to CEO, you've lost interest. Fail to see the challenge. Don't want to do it any longer.

Could it be pure paranoia? (Certainly a good reason to be on the psychologist's couch.) Too long in the workplace at the highest level. Over the years, made too many enemies.

Or in the end, might it be a simple case of workplace burnout, not so different from the guy in accounting who, eighteen months into sorting through Sarbanes-Oxley, looks ten years older and ready to be taken away in a straightjacket. The difference, however, is that corporate CEOs are substantial stockholders with large ownership stakes in their companies. They

11

don't easily change jobs or adjourn to a mental health facility as quietly as an employee in accounting.

Last but not least – could it be the anxious feeling in the pit of the stomach each time you see another CEO on the news, jacket draped across cuffed hands, taking the perp walk?

Just maybe, for Jeffrey Elkins, that was the final straw.

Breakfast Champagne

Bob Dutton was enjoying the morning sun on top of his bald and buffed head. It was such an unusually perfect day for August in the Washington metro area – blue sky, haze-free sunshine and low humidity – that he decided to forgo the AC and put the top down for his short drive to the office. God, life is good, he thought, as he turned the key and listened to the powerful V8 purr of his Alpina Roadster. Bob's house was close enough that he could walk to Easton headquarters. On some pleasant weekends when he needed to stop by the office, he trekked the two and a half miles door-to-door. But not on workdays. Part of the joy of being a senior executive was arriving in style. Give the grunts something to shoot for. Make 'em drool a little. Although Bob's military days were in his distant past, he still mentally sorted workers by rank.

Pulling out of his driveway, waving to a neighbor, Bob smiled thinking about his fine appearance. His Pelham blue Polo shirt showed off his deep tan from a full summer of golf, and also complimented the metallic silver-blue BMW. He sported Armani shades, Gucci loafers with no socks and Brooks Brothers chinos. The sun glanced off his Rolex Submariner Classic – the same model Connery wore in the Bond films.

Although not particularly tall, Bob Dutton was still in military shape from his daily weight training and running regimen. He was barrel-chested, buff, and beaming. Nothing like those pathetic looking jowly middle-aged morons driving around in their sports cars, trying to compensate for bad looks, bad breath and bad hair. Bob knew he looked good – powerful and sexy. He considered himself in the prime of his life. Three drinks into a recent night of male carousing to celebrate his fiftieth birthday, he told an old Army buddy, "Depending on their sexual orientation, people either want me, or want to be me."

Halfway to work Bob hit the brakes and made a U-turn in the middle of the lightly trafficked side street. He had just heard the announcement on the radio about the sale of the company. Gunning the engine, he let out a cowboy whoop that made the morning dog walkers on the sidewalk turn and stare.

As senior vice president of acquisitions, Dutton was the king of real estate property buy and sell in the best of Monopoly traditions. He sensed something was up at work and was experienced enough to guess what it was; but he was wise enough to keep his mouth shut. Things around the office had been a little too quiet in recent months. There were too many projects on hold. Three days ago the CEO's office quietly asked him for some sensitive statistics. He provided them without asking a single question, knowing that by not asking anything, Bob was sending the CEO a message that he understood what was developing. Then Bob went home and prayed that his assumption was correct, recognizing that if the company were acquired, he would soon be a very, very wealthy man – far beyond his wildest dreams.

And now it was like Christmas had come in August! He could barely contain himself.

The U-turn was for a quick detour to All Saints Liquors, the only area liquor store open this early in the morning. Hopping out of the car, Bob pushed through the glass doors like he was fronting an invasion. The swiftness of Bob's entrance caused the clerk to spring to his feet. The young man had been slumped on the counter in a near doze at this hour. It was too late for drunks and too early for soccer moms.

"I need three bottles of Dom, cold!" Bob barked to the clerk. While the clerk scurried off to check the cold cases, Bob perused the locked cigar display on the counter. "And gimme a dozen of these Hemingways." Tossing his company Am Ex Gold Card on the counter, he added, "Oh, yeah, and I need some cups – gimme some cups." The clerk looked puzzled but decided it would be best not to mention that the store didn't sell cups. Instead, he went in the back and pulled out a package of plastic glasses used for wine tastings, then returned to the register. Better to charge this guy five bucks for a sleeve of cups and get rid of him. Then he could return to his nap. As Bob signed the credit receipt and spun through the door with his goods, the clerk watched him climb into the expensive car.

"Jeeze, what an asshole," the clerk muttered as he returned his head to a resting position on the counter.

The Ninety Million Dollar Man

All CEOs have their quirks. Some are definitely odder than others. Money guys usually aren't "people" people. They can trend toward the ill-at-ease silent type. Jeffery Elkins fit that mold. He was good for about two minutes of small talk with strangers before he needed to move on to someone or something else. If Jeffrey had an agenda or a speech outline, a toast to deliver or a good friend at hand, he was fine – even close to normal. Otherwise, awkward.

He also had a reputation for being just a little paranoid. Health nut, germ freak, he avoided eating in public places other than the most exclusive restaurants. At catered company luncheons he moved his food around his plate but consumed nothing except the bottled water he personally opened. Within the highest levels of the company, a story became legend about Elkins' suits. Fearful of the health effects from wearing chemically dry cleaned clothes, he returned his Savile Row suits to his London tailor each spring to have the linings replaced.

From the outside – from the distance of public exposure – Elkins looked and acted the part of the consummate CEO. He definitely met the height requirement, standing just over six feet two inches. Statistics on the predominance of tall CEOs in the U.S. are well documented. He also met the good looks requirement. An attractive appearance can equate to higher pay and promotion opportunity in the workplace, regardless of job performance. Not that Jeffery Elkins wasn't equal to his peers – he fit right in – which may or may not have been a compliment in the post-ENRON era.

Jeffery liked to arrive at work soon after most employees were already at their desks. So when he parked his silver Mercedes sports coupe directly in front of the building and strode quickly through the lobby, he usually encountered only the attractive young receptionist before reaching his secluded office suite. If he had his way, there would be a private parking garage and a hidden entrance elevator directly into his office.

However, since a famous architect had designed the Easton headquarters building, the facility was already a protected landmark. It could not be altered, thanks to local preservationists. What a group, Jeffrey thought. They were hell-bent to preserve everything in the area from dirt to dilapidations, agricultural land to crumbling mansions. From a developer's perspective these people were time-consuming crazies who just didn't understand two important words: business opportunity.

Since Jeffrey Elkins couldn't change the building, he had to walk through the front doors just like every other employee. It was a morning routine that, according to the young receptionist, made him "GOA" – grumpy on arrival. On the morning the Easton sale made the news, Jeffrey felt greatly relieved knowing that he would only be required to walk through those front doors a few more times. Today the hallways weren't empty as he arrived. He sped to his office making an extra effort to avoid eye contact with anyone he passed. He didn't want to see them and he did his best not to listen. Already, there were people milling around and talking urgently in the corridors.

In his office, Jeffrey placed calls to the vice president of human resources and the security director. He wanted the VP to send out a broadcast email to division heads telling them to be in his conference room in thirty minutes. Based on the scene he observed on his way in, Jeffrey had already determined that a face-to-face meeting with employees for some kind of formal announcement was now unnecessary and unwise. The news, which had headlined the morning drive time radio airways thirty-five minutes before he arrived at his desk, was now water under the bridge. Maybe he was a coward, but he had seen some of those faces outside when he parked his car, before he had time to look away. He definitely wasn't going to address a mob of crying, angry, shocked employees and try to satisfactorily explain things. What was the point? They could read it in the papers.

Which prompted his second call. He had seen the evil looks. For all he knew someone might want him dead. And with the news breaking in tomorrow's morning editions that his cut in the deal was well over $90 million, Elkins also considered what others might want.

"Bill?" Jeffrey said into the phone after dialing the security director's number. "Do me a favor – get me a new rental car and two body guards."

Tears and Cheers

Bob Dutton sailed into the parking lot past the mourning employees without giving them a second glance. Before leaving his car in his designated parking spot, he snapped open his cell and made a tee time for an afternoon round. As he walked to his office with his briefcase in one hand and a bottle of Dom in the other, he raised the champagne as he passed a few of his fellow execs. "Come on down and let's celebrate," he said around the unlit stogie in the corner of his mouth.

In his own bliss, Bob was oblivious to the looks of anger, sadness and concern on the faces of the cubicle employees he was passing. In his office he flipped on the lights, threw his briefcase on the sofa and called for Margaret, his assistant.

"Marge, run out to my car and bring the bag of stuff from the front seat will you?" Bob was standing behind his desk, already working on opening the first bottle. He failed to glance up to see the disgusted look on Margaret's face.

"Certainly," she said coolly. Margaret had always thought of Bob as a tough straight shooter with expensive tastes and a big ego. But this morning as she walked out to his car, she was mulling over more derogatory adjectives to describe her boss. As his assistant, Margaret was the perfect counterbalance to Bob's gruff demeanor. She had the ability to make nice and smooth things over with important contacts and clients when Bob was rude or abrasive in his haste to move projects forward. Those abrasive characteristics made Bob especially good at what he did. Her primary job was to tidy up any relationship messes he left behind, and she was good at it, in her own mature, formal but friendly manner.

In the wake of this morning's news, Margaret was seeing Bob through new eyes. She didn't know whether to laugh or cry or scream when she returned to the office.

"Thanks old girl," Bob said as she walked in. Margaret put the bag of champagne, cigars and cups on his desk with a thump and shot him a stern look. For nearly a decade she'd put up with him calling her Marge instead of her actual name, but she was damned if she'd put up with "old girl."

"Careful there, Marge. That's expensive stuff!" The small group of men who had already gathered in Bob's office laughed. The first bottle was uncorked and making the rounds while the CD player blasted Beach Boys tunes.

"Anything else?" Margaret's voice had a definite edge to it, but Bob wasn't paying attention. He was busy talking and gesturing to his audience as he related his U-turn-for-champagne story and began handing out cigars. In a louder voice Margaret interrupted.

"Excuse me – Bob?" she emphasized, instead of the usual Mr. Dutton.

For the first time that morning Bob actually met her icy glare.

"What is it, Marge," he answered in his hurry-up-and-get-out-of-my-office voice.

"Congratulations," Margaret flatly intoned, locking eyes with him, in a way that made Bob feel like she had just told him to go screw himself. Then she walked out of the office and shut the door.

Jan McCarthy…

Jan McCarthy had been Norm Daniels' administrative assistant for twenty-six years – nearly half her lifetime. She was Norm's ghostwriter, editor and spell-checker long before personal computers. She picked up his dry cleaning, bought and sent flowers and cards to family members for every birthday, graduation, and christening. For two weeks each summer she was his house sitter while he went on vacation. She took in his mail, fed the pets (including the pet snake who ate the frozen mice), and on occasion paid his bills. She attended his children's weddings and even picked up a child from college in Pennsylvania one holiday weekend when Norm and his wife were traveling overseas. In her wallet she carried better photos of Norm's kids than her own. There were times when she was certain she knew his family better than he did. During those years Jan raised her own two children into young adults, but these days she found herself closer to Norm's kids than to her own. She even babysat for Norm's grandchild on the rare occasion when neighborhood sitters were unavailable.

As Jan's career at Easton progressed, she and her husband Steve drifted apart. Jan's life at work always seemed more interesting than her home life. By the time their kids were in high school, Steve had found someone more interested in him than Jan seemed to be; but Jan was oblivious.

In a two-year period, Steve left her lots of hints: suddenly scheduled late night meetings that required him to stay in the city overnight; suspicious charges on their personal credit card for purchases at Victoria's Secret; distinctively feminine perfume smells on his suits. Jan never noticed. She was too busy loving her job. In frustration and anger, Steve began blatantly writing checks from their personal account to cover the in-town condo he had rented for the now frequent overnights with his new lover. Still Jan was unaware.

Finally, Steve left one last clue for Jan. After one of his "traveling on business" weeks – he had actually been staying in the city condo – he was unpacking his suitcase on the bed at home. He pulled out his hairbrush and there it was. The evidence he was certain Jan couldn't miss. Attached to the brush were quite a few long blonde hairs. Jan, Steve and the kids all had very dark hair. Without pausing, Steve walked into the bathroom and placed the hairbrush – blonde hairs trailing – right next to Jan's toothbrush where she was sure to see it.

The next morning, Jan had just finished brushing her teeth when she noticed the hairbrush. Usually Steve kept it in the vanity drawer. As she picked it up to put it away for him, she noticed the light colored threads that were stuck in the brush. She walked to the window for a closer look. Definitely blonde hairs. Definitely. As she stared at the brush, all the other pieces of the puzzle she had been blocking out fell into place: the checks, the charges, the unusual travel patterns. Most of all how happy Steve had been for the past year. Feeling lightheaded, she sat down on the toilet seat and put her head in her hands.

"Oh God," she mumbled. "What a fool…" she began saying out loud to herself.

"You called?" whispered a voice from the bathroom doorway. She looked up and there was Steve casually leaning against the wall, looking like the happiest guy in the world.

Once the divorce was final, Jan found even more time to spend at work participating in company-sponsored events. She was the queen of corporate fundraising walks on Saturdays, soup kitchen volunteer hours on Sundays, and bake sales to benefit favorite charities. The kids now spent some weekends with their dad, which lightened her burden at home even more. Jan worked overtime as Norm moved up in the company. Her title was now executive assistant, taking on all the responsibilities that were not Norm's strengths. Details and errands, budgets and logistics, expense tracking and meeting prep just weren't Norm's thing – and never would be. So Jan learned to do them all well. Everyone who had been with the company very long knew that without Jan, Norm would be lost. Unquestionably, he knew more about planning and zoning than anyone else in the mid-Atlantic – that was his value to the organization. However, in a corporate setting, it was Jan who kept Norm functional.

On that bright blue morning, as the news about Easton slid into the drive time radio reports, Jan was already at her desk readying Norm's office for his day. There had been a flurry of data gathering activity going on recently, the kind that usually occurred whenever the company was evaluating a potential acquisition. The trinity of top execs – CEO, COO and CFO – seemed so happy this past week, Jan was certain that an announcement about the latest land acquisition by Easton would be coming soon. It made her happy too. No doubt the company's stock price would climb up a bit, which would be a good thing. Not that she owned much stock – several hundred shares in the 401(k) plan – but still, it meant that raises might be a little bigger this year.

Recently, Jan was beginning to think about retirement. She was just one year from being eligible for retiree medical coverage, the golden carrot the company dangled for long-service employees to keep them in place past mid-career. And her company pension would be waiting for her as well. As much as she loved what she did, she was starting to consider what to do with the rest of her life. Jan was certain Norm was planning to retire in a few years and she had no interest in working for anyone else.

As Jan collected Norm's schedule for the day from the printer, one of the new young finance managers walked past on the way to his office.

"Can you believe it?" he said to Jan.

"What's that?"

"They really did it. You haven't heard?"

Jan stared at him blankly. "Apparently not. What are you talking about?"

"We're being sold!"

"What? No, that can't be right. You must have heard wrong. We must be buying…"

But the young man disrespectfully cut her off before she could finish. "I'm positively right," he emphasized. "It was on WTOP. Pratt-Miles is buying us for $13 billion." And with that he turned and walked on to spread the news to the next unsuspecting soul he encountered. Jan stood shell-shocked, mouth agape, as Norm's schedule fluttered from her hand.

First Responders

No other East Coast office building looked quite like The Easton Company's headquarters. Built in the 1960s, it was an architectural oddity that people either loved or hated. The architect would later become world-renowned, but in the '60s he was still designing gas stations, so it was easy to debate whether the Easton building was an architectural gem of any significance. The front of the building facing the road was a two story series of white stucco boxes bedecked with irregularly placed balconies, a scattering of pyramid skylights, and a small grove of trees growing on the rooftop terraces. The back of the building rose three stories from ground level. Glass walls faced a man-made lake surrounded by mature trees and a landscaped walking path.

The adjoining lakefront property included several restaurants, a sailing dock, bell tower, fountain, sculpture gardens and stage area. The locale was known for its schedule of outdoor community events. Throughout the year the lakefront was a regional venue for concerts, fundraisers, fairs, competitions, boat races, movies and holiday celebrations. Today, however, the event taking shape around the headquarters building was a solemn one.

As Kate Cooper pulled into the parking lot she saw small groups of people clustered under the trees. Some were crying. Others were embracing. Most looked upset or shocked. It was a beautiful late-summer sunny morning but the faces of the employees gathered outside were clouded by grief.

...With the Scissors, In the Corner Office

By the time Norm Daniels parked his silver Audi sedan in the side parking lot at The Easton Company building, it was after 9 a.m. Not much of a talker, Norm was hoping to slip unnoticed through a side door and get to his office without a great deal of conversation along the way. There would be plenty of time in the coming weeks to beat to death the topic at hand – the sale of The Easton Company. He wanted no part of that this morning.

Although soon to be one of the newly-minted Easton Company multimillionaires, Norm was having trouble locating the joy in this news. He liked his life the way it was and he wasn't sure he really wanted to trade it away for a boatload of cash and parting gifts. He was comfortable in his roles and responsibilities at work and at home. He enjoyed his career and his routine, which included twenty laps at the health club pool each morning before work, a Caribou decaf with his Wall Street Journal, tuna salad at lunch, and a quick stop for a light beer with his local government contact every third Thursday evening before scheduled zoning meetings. His niche, planning and zoning, was boring fare compared to the more glitzy stuff his peers at Easton worked on. But that was okay with Norm. He liked finite. He enjoyed undemanding repetition. The only people who ever got excited about zoning were the Not In My Back Yard crowd who changed with the project and the seasons.

The other part of his life that Norm dearly treasured was the experience of being well cared for. The existence of an executive at a Fortune 500 company can be meaningful in different ways to different people. Norm had no real interest in country club memberships, five star travel, or the extravagant expense account at his disposal. Even the beautiful panoramic lakefront view from his windowed corner office failed to impress him. Instead, Norm treasured not having to deal with all of life's minor irritations, expectations

23

and normal demands. For him, that was the most valuable executive privilege. He loved not being bothered by the world of car maintenance, dry cleaners, plumbers, bill paying, grocery shopping, lawn care, schedule juggling, tax preparation, estate planning, child care, car pools, finding the best physicians, making dinner reservations, or even resetting the clocks throughout his house twice a year. In one way or another, those things and many others were all taken care of for him. Some of them were company perks. Some were handled by his wife. The rest were things Jan had taken off his plate over the years as part of her responsibilities as his executive assistant. That left Norm free to be Norm. It was a great life.

As Norm closed his office door and settled into the comfortable leather chair behind his desk, he sported a smug smile. He was quite pleased with himself. He had successfully traveled from the parking lot to the third floor with no more than a few head nods required of him along the way. What luck, Norm thought. Even Jan was away from her desk. He was home free.

Just as Norm closed his office door, Jan returned from the ladies room. She had been there since that idiot finance manager dumped the news on her about the sale of the company. She couldn't believe this was happening. She couldn't believe she had gotten the news from some insensitive young snot who didn't even know her name. Locked in the far bathroom stall, red-faced and crying, it had taken her all this time and an entire roll of toilet paper to control her furious anger and harness her tears. She felt betrayed, wasted, unappreciated and unloved. But most of all she was really, really angry. When Jan finally got her breathing back to normal, she blotted her face with wet paper towels and then attempted to reapply some make-up.

Walking back to her desk Jan felt empty and fragile, but she believed she had her emotions sufficiently in check. As she put her purse on her desk, she looked up and noticed Norm in his office, looking the same as he looked every other morning, reviewing the schedule she had prepared for him as though nothing had changed.

A few seconds later, Norm looked up from the daily schedule in his hand to see Jan coming though his door.

"Good morn..."

Before Norm could finish, Jan moved swiftly around his desk.

"Why you sonofabitch...!" she screeched, leaning over him, her right hand raised in a fist above her head as though she was about to strike him.

It was pure reflex that made Norm reach up and grab Jan's forearm. And it was only then that he glanced up and saw the pair of scissors in her fist.

24

Get the Hell Out!

The party in Bob's office was going full throttle by 10 a.m. Cigars were lit – even though the building was nonsmoking – the champagne was nearly gone and Bob's mates were dancing and singing surf tunes in between loud and raucous conversations about living large with newfound wealth.

When Margaret walked out of Bob's office an hour earlier, she headed directly to the executive suite and into Lee Martino's office.

Lee had joined the company two years earlier as Easton's chief operating officer. His arrival prompted the retirement of senior company executives, each of whom might have been the next CEO if Jeffrey ever decided to retire. All three men had spent their careers at Easton and were serious businessmen. But when Jeffrey brought in Lee Martino and named him the new COO without discussion, the writing on the wall was clear. Lee was the new heir apparent waiting to take over The Easton Company when Jeffrey decided to step down.

What employees liked most about Lee was his pleasant personality. He wasn't a snob like many of Easton's senior executives. Clearly, Lee appreciated the good life and quietly took full advantage of the company's executive perks. The difference was that he didn't flaunt such things in the presence of lower level employees. Lee treated all his coworkers with respect. He was a busy man but never too busy to say hello, or stop and talk for a few minutes. When Margaret entered Lee's office, he had just arrived at his desk and was sliding his suit jacket onto the back of his chair.

"Excuse me, Mr. Martino. I know it's a busy morning…"

Lee couldn't help but chuckle at Margaret Warner's businesslike demeanor and tone. "Yes, it certainly is Margaret. It's going to be a very busy time for many of us over the next few months. What can I do for you?" he smiled politely but continued standing behind his desk.

"A small favor. It's about decorum. When you have a minute, could you drop by Bob's office? I'd appreciate your feedback on something."

Before Lee could ask any questions, Margaret turned and left. Lee made some phone calls and attended a short meeting in the CEO's office with their two executive secretaries. The intent was to provide instructions regarding which calls Jeffrey and Lee would and would not be taking that day, and how to handle inquiries from the press and other outsiders. In return, the secretaries talked about the employees' reaction to the announcement. Lee's assistant, Beverly, was straightforward in her comments.

"You need to understand how upset we all are. People are in shock. They're crying and calling their shrinks."

Sitting behind his desk, Jeffrey continued making notes and didn't look up. "No doubt their lives will be a bit disrupted for a little while," he murmured in a detached tone.

Jeffrey's apparent lack of interest made Lee uncomfortable. Lee added, "Okay. We'll be sensitive to that. Thanks for letting us know."

Walking down the corridor to Bob's office, Lee could hear the music before he turned the corner. The chorus of "Surfin' Safari" filled the hallway. Margaret looked up from her desk and then glanced pointedly toward Bob's door. Inside Bob and Ray Palmer had their shoes off, pants legs rolled up, and were dancing the swim on top of Bob's desk. At least a dozen other party participants crammed the smoke filled room. Without hesitating, Lee swung the door open and walked in.

"Hey good buddy," Bob said loudly over the music when he saw Lee. Lee slammed the door shut behind him.

"Turn off the music," Lee enunciated in a low commanding voice. A few of the execs in the room read the anger on Lee's face and one reached over and touched the pause button on the CD player.

"Get out. All of you, out." Lee seethed.

"What the hell?" Bob shouted as he hopped down off the desk.

"Let's get this straight," Lee continued, all six feet five inches of his body rigidly leaning forward, his eyes burning down into Bob's face. It was quite clear whom he was addressing. "This is not a bar. This is not a frat party. This is still The Easton Company and your place of employment. I want you out. Get out of this office. Get out of this building. Get the hell out and don't come back until you can conduct yourself professionally. And if you can't do that, then don't bother."

"What the...?" Bob began again, but Lee already had his hand on the doorknob.

He looked back at Bob one more time and said, "I mean it! Get the hell out!"

Twenty minutes later Bob and most of his entourage had reconvened at the hotel restaurant across the street from Easton's offices. Occupying the large leather upholstered corner booth, the mood was more subdued than it had been in Bob's office but the group was still noisy and happy as they ordered Bloody Marys and assigned foursomes for the afternoon's golf outing.

"Hey men." Bob injected, his commanding officer voice interrupting the conversations around him. "A toast!" They raised their glasses. "To fun and freedom!" The group laughed and clinked glasses. "I do believe we have been released. Let's get the hell out of here and go hit some balls."

And so it went for the next thirteen weeks. A majority of Easton's mostly male upper management arrived late at the office – if at all – took long lunches and left early for the golf course when weather permitted.

Meanwhile, in human resources, the legal department, the finance and accounting divisions – men and women alike were present from start to finish every day since the burden of merger work weighed heaviest upon their areas. Administrative staff and secretaries, mail clerks and the maintenance crew, along with most of Easton's female employees – whether receptionists or senior vice presidents – arrived early to work, searched the internet for new jobs, and talked among themselves about daily developments in the merger process.

Moods among workers continued to ramble from anger and disbelief, to sarcasm and sorrow. On some days, employees cared passionately about their work at The Easton Company. Other days, they felt detached and were careless about the work on their desks. Some cried regularly. Others took long lunches. Most everyone stopped working past five o'clock, unless specifically asked to stay. These dependable people were the employees who kept the business of The Easton Company functioning while the new owners waited to take over. In the wake of the announcement of sale, these were the employees who asked, "What are we supposed to be doing?" The answer came back, "Just keep doing what you've always done until someone instructs you otherwise." So they did.

But during the weeks between the announcement and the executed sale of the company, there was an inverse relationship between an employee's sense of job responsibility and their total compensation. Those who were working hardest were generally the lowest paid, and they were about to get the short end of the stick when the company was sold.

Bad Timing

Tim Ferris was the last senior management employee hired before the Easton sale was announced. He had given up a lucrative position with an international company six times the size of Easton to take charge of Easton's audit function.

At age thirty-one, Tim and his wife had recently become parents for the first time. Their twin boys were born prematurely but had grown into very healthy ten-month-olds. Living through those stressful weeks of the boys' hospitalization in the neonatal unit was just enough incentive for Tim to take a clear-eyed look at his job and his life and determine that a little more balance was in order. Following a short job search, he landed the position at Easton. The new job paid slightly more than his previous one and required less travel; and The Easton Company seemed family friendly – something he had not previously considered when evaluating employers. Still, Tim had given up advancement opportunities and bigger bonus potential at the larger organization to come to a smaller one. When he made his decision to change employers, the trade-offs seemed to make sense. With two infants in the family he was certain the move would be worth it in the long run.

For six months life was good and Tim was happy. Then came the merger announcement. He was on his way to work that morning when he ran over some debris in the road that shredded his left rear tire and forced him to pull onto the shoulder. Tim decided to change the tire instead of waiting the better part of an hour for AAA to show up. It was a beautiful August day, but it was still August in Washington – too hot to be changing a tire in a suit and tie. He had an important meeting with outside vendors on his morning schedule. Now here he was on the roadside, his white shirt wrinkled and stained with perspiration, and black marks on his rolled sleeves.

That morning Tim was driving the family car since his MG was in the shop again. With the tire finally changed, he searched the car and rummaged in the trunk for a towel or a rag or anything on which to wipe his hands and face. There was nothing except a few infant size disposable diapers in the twins' auxiliary diaper bag. He contemplated whether to limp the car back home on the donut spare and change clothes or continue on to work and attempt to clean himself up before the vendors meeting. As he was wiping his face with a tiny Huggies disposable diaper, Tim's cell phone rang. Answering the call, he received the news about the sale of The Easton Company.

It was Ben Morgan on the phone, one of his new friends and the chief information officer at Easton. Although both men were division heads, neither Tim nor Ben had received any advance notice about the sale. Hearing the news on his car radio, Ben immediately called Tim.

"Oh God," Tim moaned. "This can't be happening."

"It makes me want to throw a brick through Elkins' window," Ben growled. "We've both been with Easton less than a year so we're definitely screwed, man."

Tim could feel his blood pressure rising. "OK. Look, I'll catch you later today. I need to get going here."

"Right. No problem," Ben replied. "We need a strategy. But first we need more information. See you later in the office."

Tim snapped shut his cell phone and threw it into the trunk of the car along with the sopping Huggie he had been clutching in his other hand. He climbed into the driver's seat and headed home. Under these new circumstances, he'd be damned if he was going to work for a meeting with potential new vendors, even if they were Jeffrey Elkins' golfing buddies. He would alert his secretary to call and cancel, or if they were already sitting in the lobby, send them on their way. And no, he would not be rescheduling, he thought as he anticipated his secretary's questions.

At that moment, what angered Tim most was realizing he had given up a very demanding but good career with his former employer. In its place he was now in a position to be laid off after half a year in his new job. As he guided the gimpy car back toward home Tim pounded the steering wheel and ranted out loud, "Damn it, someone has some explaining to do!"

29

Taking Care of Business

Bing Sullivan had a reputation for being an extremely fun individual. As senior vice president of marketing for The Easton Company, Bing often bragged to friends and relatives that he had the best job in the whole corporation – he got to think up crazy ideas and go out to play with the clients.

Bing was the longtime marketing genius behind Easton's new property rollouts. He knew how to put together the right mix of flash, splash and wow-factor to ensure a successful grand opening. Over-the-top was usually just the beginning when Bing was involved. His address book included entries for the Ohio State Marching Band, Cindi Crawford, the CEOs of FTD and Balloons Over America, the manager of the Dallas Cowboys cheerleaders, the IATSE (International Alliance of Theatrical Stage Employees), Rod Stewart, and the Ringling Bros. Circus.

At fifty-six, Bing had seen it all, done it all, and was ready to do it all again. He was always on the go. Bing's colleagues swore he couldn't sit still for more than eight consecutive minutes. Bing rode his Harley and wore his favorite leather jacket to work every day – and he claimed the jacket was the original worn by Brando in *The Wild One*, acquired at a Christie's auction.

Over the years Bing had lived his job. He still put in a lot of hours, but these days he spent most of his time traveling around the country entertaining clients and spending his massive travel and entertainment budget. His expenses, however, trended toward the nontraditional. His was not the land of dinner, drinks and theater tickets. If you were the type of client who expected to be entertained at the best restaurants in town, Bing would line you up with one of his senior marketing reps. He would see to your happiness, but you were definitely not his type. On an outing with Bing, you were more likely to hit the best barbeque spot in the area, drive race cars together at the regional NASCAR track, and then visit a small but energetic bar on the outskirts of town with the best local bands and outstanding home brews on tap. If you were one of Bing's clients, spending time with him was like getting caught up in a small tornado. There was no stopping Bing once he got going and if you were on his calendar, you were going with him. He had talked clients into everything from hang gliding lessons to Karaoke performances.

Once, when Easton's director of risk management had approached Bing with his concerns about the liability the company was taking on in Bing's entertainment budget, Bing just smiled and slapped the guy on the back.

"Not to worry, Chris. I haven't lost a client yet."

Conversations like this one were always on the go. If you wanted to talk to Bing about anything, you had to be a fast walker and a short talker. You had to catch up with him as he was walking by, walk at his fast pace long enough to have your conversation, and finish it before Bing reached his office door or his motorcycle, depending on whether he was coming or going.

Bing's enthusiasm for whatever he was working on was so contagious he could convince almost anyone to do nearly anything. He was the person who convinced Don Asher, one of Easton's senior executives, to dress in drag for a fashion show fundraiser long ago. Back then, some of his peers couldn't believe Bing had managed to talk Don into doing it – some even believed it had cost Don a shot at the CEO slot – but Bing's response was straightforward.

"Hell, that was one of the easiest sells I've ever made. What guy wouldn't want to get into a dressing room with the hottest young models from New York's legendary Ford modeling agency."

When anyone asked Bing why he enjoyed marketing so much, he explained that the job let him try on different hats. He meant that both figuratively and literally. Bing had a weakness for anything that involved wearing a costume or uniform, or using some special equipment. Whenever he had an opportunity to try out something for the first time, he usually managed to walk away with some part of – if not all of – the garb and gizmos. A sampling of the stuff in his closet at home included outfits for Texas line dancing (he especially loved the boots he had gotten in Austin); his parachute pack from his first solo jump; a laser gun smuggled from a laser tag arena; a clown costume; NASCAR jacket; stethoscope and black doctor's bag (embossed with someone else's gold initials); a hang-gliding helmet; a putter from Arnie's bag; a Taser from a police ride-along program; his flight suit from sitting in the copilot's seat of an F-16 jet; even an autographed apron Emeril had given him to wear during a cooking show.

But his favorite keepsake, as he referred to his acquisitions, was the Elvis costume he once wore at an impersonators contest in Las Vegas. For Bing, there was something extra special about all those rhinestones on white leather

31

with the yards of fringe, the white silk scarf, and the gold Elvis aviator sunglasses with *EP* molded in the nose-bridge and TCB on the arms.

Bing was in the thick of directing the setup for a grand opening in La Jolla when he got the call about the sale of the company. He was standing amidst a white chaos that in twenty-four hours would be a full-scale snow-tubing venue with a Christmas in August theme. The freezer trucks and snowmaking equipment were rumbling loudly in the background when he took the call from Lee Martino, Easton's chief operating officer.

"For real?" he shouted into his cell when Lee told him the merger news had hit the wires three hours earlier on the East Coast.

"You'll be needed back here on Monday morning for the change in control group meeting." Lee informed him.

"Anything else I need to know before then?" Bing asked.

"It's going to be a short timeline. Pratt-Miles wants to close in less than twelve weeks."

"Guess I better start looking for a new job," Bing joked.

"Probably not necessary. It's not like you'll be pressed for cash you know."

"Yeah, but I'm not ready to walk the beach 24/7 just yet either," Bing replied. "Maybe it's time I called Jeff Gordon about those driving lessons he's been promising me."

Lee laughed and told Bing he would see him on Monday.

"And do us all a favor, Bing. Don't decide to go over Niagara Falls in a barrel between now and then."

In the News – Cotton Candy Stock Market

Closing Market Summary – August 14

The Easton Company (NYSE-TEC), +22.02 to $55.12, signed a definitive merger agreement with **Pratt-Miles** (NYSE-PMI), -$2.97 to $28.04. Each share of Easton will be exchanged for $65.00 in cash. The transaction is expected to close in the fourth quarter.

The stock market had been climbing for weeks. Financial pundits continued to debate what was really driving the rise. In a post-9/11 culture, many simply labeled it a continued recovery and left it at that. Still, in the calendar year that The Easton Company was acquired, the number of mergers and acquisitions in the U.S. increased by forty-six percent. For better or for worse, all those mergers were pumping a certain amount of air and spun sugar into particular segments of the market.

Most of these marriages of industry were not being consummated out of love, admiration and mutual respect. In the case of hostile takeovers, they were no more than shotgun weddings. Many mergers were arranged unions brokered by powerful business families, driven by the big dowry of one corporation and the covetous urgency of another.

Productivity gains? Profit growth? Economic growth? Fact-based market optimism? None of these could claim credit for the upward market spiral. The primary influence was all those takeovers. The availability of large sums of cash inside many corporations coupled with low interest loans had spurred companies to go shopping. As mergers were announced within a sector, investors raced to buy stock in similar businesses, viewing those same sector companies as potentially "in play." Such buying frenzy drove stock prices higher, based on nothing more than hopeful speculation. Competitive debt on company balance sheets became more acceptable to investors, and the next thing anyone knew – zoom – off to the stock market races.

Attentive investors know that when these situations occur the process just keeps repeating itself until some voice in the wilderness spouts a timely, "Hey, wait a minute. Where's the higher productivity, new products, increased efficiency, etc. to back all this up?" Uh-oh. What follows is euphemistically referred to as a correction.

Clearly, the initiation of The Easton Company's merger with Pratt-Miles was in the midst of one of these cotton candy, spun sugar market cycles.

PART TWO

A GLANCE BACK IN TIME

A Clandestine Game of Pick-Up Sticks

Fletcher Johnston became a millionaire before his thirty-second birthday. As a young attorney fresh out of law school, Fletcher joined his father's law firm. Fletcher's charismatic good looks and demeanor, combined with the firm's established name and reputation, made him popular with his father's clients. He quickly became *the* divorce attorney to high profile clients in Georgetown and the Virginia hunt country – clients who were willing to pay generously to settle affairs quietly with attorneys who didn't leak stories to the Washington press. In his first five years of practice Fletcher doubled the earnings of the family's thirty-year-old law firm.

But it was his father's sudden death that made Fletcher a millionaire. In the early hours of an unforgettably cold Monday in February, Fletcher discovered his father's body slumped over West's Annotated Code of Virginia. A widower, his father often went to work on weekends when the office was quiet. Sadly, he had expired with no one around to find him until Fletcher opened the senior partner's office door. The old man died of a massive stroke while sitting at his desk, leaving Fletcher the firm and his amassed fortune.

Six weeks after the funeral, Fletcher named himself partner emeritus, sold controlling interest in the firm to the remaining senior partners and left town. There were lots of ways to kill oneself, but working to death was not a choice Fletcher wanted to inherit.

Leaving behind his brief but successful work history, Fletcher spent the next eighteen months following every boyhood whim he'd ever imagined, including his dream of skiing the highest slopes in Europe. He drank martinis and played roulette in Monaco, lounged on the Med's elite topless beaches, hung out with artists on the Cote D'Or, and ate his way through the Michelin starred restaurants in Paris. When Bobby Kennedy was assassinated the

37

American jet-set tide in Europe ebbed stateside, and it seemed the days of Camelot were truly coming to a close. Fletcher followed the flow and returned home. Using his previous Georgetown connections, he took a position as a corporate attorney for a small but growing development company. On his first day working for the new employer, Fletcher stowed his snow skis behind his office door as a reminder to make time to play.

And play he did, but not on the ski slopes. Fletcher's new responsibilities focused on land deals – an area he had dabbled in as an offshoot of his divorce practice for a handful of his clients – buying and selling rural real estate in the Virginia countryside. Land deals were easy compared to divorce settlements. To Fletcher these land development deals seemed like child's play – a mix of capture the flag, red rover, Jenga, and hide-and-seek. He loved all the planning and pretense that led up to the surreptitious parcel purchases. Researching land records and analyzing owners made him feel like a detective or a secret operative. The challenge of buying up land quietly and quickly reminded him of an undercover version of pick-up sticks.

By the time The Easton Company made its announcement to the residents of northern Virginia that it would build a new city in the rural landscape west of the nation's capital, Fletcher had managed to successfully accumulate for his employer 15,000 acres from 150 separate owners. It helped that the landowners Fletcher was dealing with were unfamiliar with his employer. Fletcher and his growing staff had done a good job of stealthily acquiring a number of large tracts before anyone got suspicious. But in the five months preceding the release of development plans by Ed Easton, the company's owner, the community was rife with rumor and speculation. The cat was out of the bag; residents just didn't have any idea what the cat actually looked like. So Ed's announcement about building a new concept city from scratch put to rest various rumors which had run rampant through the rural community: that the mysterious land acquisition was for a giant amusement park, a nuclear waste facility, or a secret bio-lab to study highly infectious diseases. Then, near the end of the initial land acquisition process, as the natives realized a single buyer was purchasing all this land, conspiracy theories started to circulate. The most popular one asserted that Russian communists were attempting to establish a foothold near Washington, D.C.

Fletcher was proud of his accomplishments. He had acquired a large portion of the land for less than $1,000 an acre and managed to keep the average per acre price to $1,500, with the last sellers getting nearly double what the first ones were paid just twenty months prior.

As it turned out, this would end up being the most exciting period of Fletcher's career, although he didn't know it at the time. He had made plenty of new friends as he swapped stories with, entertained, hunted with, dined with, rode with, drank with, sang with, and got to know a large percentage of the families in the vicinity. He had attended a funeral and two weddings and managed to evade three matchmaking schemes with landowners' available young daughters These people liked Fletcher and he liked them.

Of course the friendships couldn't last and most dissolved before Ed Easton's announcement was made. When people found out what the future of their valley was going to look like, they were both relieved (the Russians weren't really coming) and angry. Fletcher was no longer a popular guy.

When he received the first death threat, he turned it over to the authorities and shrugged it off. Two weeks later a man with a shotgun – someone Fletcher had never seen before – appeared at his car window outside a local diner late one night and suggested Fletcher leave the area, permanently. The next day, after a call to the local sheriff and a brief meeting with his staff and then Ed Easton. Fletcher departed for a sabbatical in California to research some developable land in Simi Valley.

Upon his eventual return to the Washington area, Fletcher Johnston continued to work for The Easton Company until the day it was sold, but he never lived anywhere near the new city Ed was building. Instead, he established residence in the District of Columbia, buying a brand new condo in The Watergate.

Over the years, orchestrating new land deals around the country made time fly for Fletcher. His job with Easton grew along with the company. He often looked back fondly on his eighteen-month European travel break from employment. Even though he took an annual vacation, it was usually in August when business in the mid-Atlantic area slowed to a crawl and workaholics weren't missed at their desks. So the snow skis stayed behind his office door and became more symbolic than functional as the years slipped by.

Simple Truths

Reviewing a corporation's prospectus can often leave the reader in doubt about what the company actually does, and generally provides no clue regarding the organization's definition for business success. When Ed Easton founded The Easton Company, he made it clear to those who chose to invest their time, talents, and money exactly how he measured success. He put it in writing and signed his name to it for all to see:

Like people, companies have personalities. Some are alert and efficient, others are sluggish and clumsy; some are warm and friendly, others are cold and self-centered. Personality is not an accident. It depends upon what goes on inside the person – or the company. "What does he live for?" "What does she want?" And with a company: "What's its purpose?" "What are its goals?"

- The answers aren't easy for a person or a company. However, the goals of a truly successful company might be these:
- To provide a useful service or product
- To provide thoughtfully for the people who spend their days at work in it
- To produce a profit

You can't put these in any order of priority. Each is indispensable to overall success. Each of us in the company must keep his eye on each of these goals and chase them hard if we are to have the kind of company we really want.

40

We are fortunate that the very nature of our business so directly involves service to the community. We help build homes, stores, office buildings, factories, and all kinds of facilities that are important to the health, growth and vitality of a community. As a company, therefore, we will fulfill the first goal if we just do our jobs outstandingly well.

The second goal requires much of a company: fair salaries, pleasant working conditions, opportunities for growth and advancement, friendly associates, and continuing concern for the welfare of each individual in the company.

We cannot fail in the third goal for very long and stay in business, but if we can't achieve the first two goals, and also earn a profit we are in the wrong business – our service isn't really needed. On the other hand, if our business has the potential for useful service which we believe ours does; if the company cares about each of us the way it should and if we give back the same kind of concern about every detail of the company's operations, then profits are bound to follow – for the company and for each of us who works in it.

Popular archived photos of Ed Easton show a portly gentleman in a rumpled madras sports coat wearing horn-rimmed glasses. In the photos he is happily cutting cake and distributing slices to young and old at the company's annual community birthday celebration. Looking back, outsiders might say Ed's business doctrine was just the lofty ideals of a dreamer in the 1960s. However, for those who personally experienced working for Ed, it was the real deal.

The CEO Who Didn't Love It Enough To Keep It

In the nearly fifty-year history of The Easton Company there were three CEOs: the Visionary Founder; the Pensive Caretaker; and the One Who Didn't Love It Enough to Keep It. According to the Friends of The Easton Company, Jeffrey Elkins was the lowest of the lot. He was the CEO who didn't love the company enough to keep it. Following the merger announcement, "Friends of The Easton Company" was the label Jeffrey Elkins sarcastically used when referring to members of the press, Easton employees, and people in the community who, after years of varying support and criticism, suddenly had an undying love for all things Easton.

As the initial shock of becoming *persona non grata* in his own company began to wear off, Elkins gave up any remaining pretense of caring what anyone thought of him. When he arrived at work accompanied by two bodyguards the week after the merger announcement, some employees actually had the nerve to talk about his behavior within earshot.

"Bodyguards," one secretary sneered. "He's bringing bodyguards into one of the friendliest companies in America. Ed Easton must be spinning in his grave."

She was right of course, Jeffrey thought. Ed Easton had been many things to many people – founder, visionary, and consensus builder – but to describe his personality nearly everyone used words like friendly, down home, accessible, and genuine. There would have been no place for bodyguards in Ed Easton's world. Yes, Ed had been trusting and trustworthy, but certainly not charismatic. Like many very intelligent people, he was oblivious to his personal appearance: overweight, wearing outdated eyeglasses and recycling the same sports coat and two stained ties all season long. In Ed's case it was his caring eyes and his friendly smile along with his brilliant ideas that made the man – not his clothes or his physique. Still, thought Jeffrey, if Ed Easton

42

were alive and leading the company, he probably would have run the place into the ground by now. Sure he was trusted and loved, but he was no businessman – at least not like Jeffrey. Easton was just too nice a guy; too focused on the whole social ethics thing. The concept of watching out for the good of all mankind just didn't have a place in the for-profit world – at least not in this era.

In fact, the need for more acute business acumen had been a decisive factor when Ed Easton transitioned to chairman emeritus and Andrew Heath took over as CEO. Andrew had been the company's chief legal counsel. He was a quiet man – very cerebral. But he also had a quick temper that showed itself infrequently yet memorably. His anger was absolutely not something you wanted to experience first hand – and definitely not more than once in a lifetime. Andrew had been chosen to lead the company because his contract negotiating skills and land lease/purchase strategies were both cunning and cutting-edge. The Easton board of directors agreed unanimously that Andrew Heath was the right CEO to grow the company to the next level of land and property holdings. He held the position for nine years, until he turned sixty-five.

When the time came for Andrew to announce his retirement, there were three possible inside candidates for CEO and they each wanted the job.

Jeffrey Elkins had proven himself as the serious numbers guy who knew when a deal made financial sense and when it didn't. He would walk away from what others saw as an attractive opportunity when he couldn't make the financials look as good as the property – and he had never been wrong. Elkins was legend for his unwavering good business sense.

At the other end of the spectrum, Don Asher had earned his reputation as Easton's community liaison. Don was friendly and gregarious. He golfed with developers and played tennis with residential builders. He was the person to know if you needed tickets to a Redskins playoff game or a sold-out Jimmy Buffet concert. It was Don's picture that appeared in the papers presenting the latest big check corporate contribution to a local foundation or nonprofit. And it was Don who willingly participated in area fundraisers as speaker, auctioneer, or master of ceremonies. Once he even dressed in drag for a fashion show to raise money for a good cause. Which, in the end, is exactly why everyone knew the next Easton CEO wouldn't be Don Asher. He was fluff, not substance.

Simon Miller was the executive to watch at The Easton Company. If Don Asher was the guy everyone wanted to hang out with, Simon Miller was the person everyone else wanted to emulate, work for and see succeed. He was well loved and respected. Of the three candidates for next CEO, Simon was the one who actually lived in the local community. He was active in his children's schools and activities, his church, and in a long list of community organizations – not because he felt he had to be there for his job, but because he loved his community, his work, and the founder of the company he worked for. It was Simon who had inherited the company vision from Ed Easton. Simon was wise and compassionate. He was the champion of good causes; and among his fellow executives Simon was the sole advocate for company employees.

Everyone looked first to Simon when there was a company-wide issue to be decided. He had the best global perspective for advancing projects and resolving problems. From the seats around the board table, Simon was the obvious choice for succession. After all, Jeffrey could continue supplying the acute business insight even after Simon was named the new CEO.

Of course Jeffrey didn't see it that way. In his mind Simon was too sensitive; wore his heart on his sleeve too frequently. In fact, in Jeffrey's opinion, Simon was too much like Ed, putting employees and the community first and stockholders second. That sort of thinking was for nonprofits, not publicly held corporations like The Easton Company. Jeffrey knew that no one had any particularly warm feelings toward him. Still, he saw himself as the logical choice. With the recent growth in the company's holdings, it was time to turn Easton into a serious profit maker and he was the person to do it.

Weeks went by, providing the candidates plenty of schmoozing opportunity with board members at exclusive locations. All indications were pointing to Simon Miller as the next Easton CEO, and Jeffery could feel the sea change in his dealings with his peers and the board. Still there was no announcement about Andrew's successor.

Then a terrible thing happened:

EASTON HEAD SIMON MILLER DIES IN CRASH

WASHINGTON (FNS) – Simon R. Miller, 47, president of The Easton Company, died early Friday morning when his private plane crashed near Atlanta.

According to an Easton spokesman, the plane suffered engine failure and crashed near Atlanta's DeKalb-Peachtree Airport. Miller had been vacationing on Jekyll Island over the Labor Day Weekend with his family and was returning to Washington for a business meeting when his plane went down. No one on the ground was injured....

The company and the community went into mourning. Everyone had loved Simon Miller and he had been authentically involved in the fabric of his community – the same community that The Easton Company had founded and developed. The local obituaries ran with the assumption that Simon Miller would have been Easton's next CEO. Amidst the eulogizing, Jeffrey

Elkins could barely contain his anger; however, he quickly concluded that he was now the only obvious choice for CEO succession. After Simon's private funeral, his family held a very public memorial service that had to be rescheduled at an outdoor location because no auditorium, church or other venue in the community was large enough to hold the anticipated crowd of mourners.

Following a full month of silence on the topic, Andrew Heath postponed his retirement for a year before unceremoniously turning the company over to Jeffrey with the board's blessing. During that year an elementary school, a street and a library were renamed for Simon Miller, and within twenty-six months the Simon R. Miller Endowed Chair of Community Development was established at the University of Virginia. Jeffrey took charge of The Easton Company feeling both overlooked and underappreciated by all, and some portion of those emotions never left him.

Fifteen years after the tragedy, the Friends of The Easton Company couldn't help but revisit what might have been. What if Simon Miller had lived instead of dying in that plane crash? Certainly, Elkins would never have become CEO, and the sale of The Easton Company would never have happened.

A Gift From Ed

Ed Easton was still chairman emeritus when Jeffrey Elkins was named CEO of The Easton Company. On that day, Jeffrey received a hand-delivered linen envelope with "Jeffrey" penned in green ink across the front. Inside the envelope he found a formal note card with the phrase "a line from Ed" embossed in the lower right hand corner. The message within was written in Ed Easton's distinctive green felt-tip scrawl:

> *Congratulations and all good wishes for the continued success of the company. Don't screw it up.*
>
> *– Ed*
>
> *P.S. I'm having a little something special made for you to mark the occasion. It will be along in a while. Hope you enjoy it.*

Although curious about the "something special," when nothing arrived that week Jeffrey decided whatever Ed had contemplated sending had slipped the old man's mind.

Fifteen weeks later, Jeffrey's secretary received an overseas phone call. It was from a furniture company in Milan advising that a special order for Jeffery Elkins was ready to ship. The shipment was scheduled to arrive in the States in about ten days via white glove delivery. At first Jeffery was certain the message must be a mistake. He had Gloria, his secretary, call back to confirm. It was then Gloria learned the order had been placed by Ed Easton. No doubt some odd little lamp or unique writing desk, Jeffrey thought. That would be the kind of thing Ed would choose to send.

In the weeks after Jeffrey became CEO, his wife's New York interior designer had decorated his new office. It contained a wonderful collection of eclectic but tasteful eighteenth-century post-colonial and western expansion American furnishings appropriate for an executive suite. Jeffrey chose to display a few favorite pieces of original art from The Easton Company's art and artifacts collection. In particular, two original Leroy Neimans added a touch of excitement and color to the otherwise staid décor.

Jeffrey was out of town when Ed's gift arrived. Gloria was appalled when the deliverymen carted the huge crate into Jeffery's office. She cautioned the unpackers to use care not to disturb or mar the other fine antique pieces already placed in the room. Once the packing materials were taken away and the men departed, what remained was a small, custom-made Italian leather sofa.

The piece was from the Galaxy line of a top name Italian furniture designer – a throwback to 1960s modern styling. The supple leather was of the highest quality in a pale shade of butter yellow. The sofa sat where the movers had placed it – angled off to the right of Jeffrey's desk, wedged between a Hepplewhite sideboard and a Goddard tea table.

Gloria felt ill just looking at the thing. It reminded her of a melting block of reused lard. When Don Asher, Easton's community liaison executive, walked by Jeffrey's office he joked that the sofa looked like an Italian designer's interpretation of Captain Kirk's chair on the Enterprise. Like much European furniture, the sofa appeared invitingly comfortable but in reality it was painful to occupy. The sofa cushions nearly swallowed any occupant and it required a helping hand to free oneself. Don Asher, trying it out at Gloria's request, found himself seated with his knees close to his ears. As if the sofa's design wasn't atrocious enough, Ed had arranged to have the Easton logo branded into the back cushion, which made the thing hideous.

Pushing himself up out of the sofa, Don's hand slipped between the cushions and he extracted a small envelope, unaddressed and unsealed. Assuming it to be part of the delivery paperwork he handed it to Gloria. Inside was a one-by-two inch newspaper clipping with just a few lines of type. Nothing else. Gloria's face went white as she scanned it. Without saying a word she handed it back to Don. The clipping read:

If there are ways for CEOs to go to jail, it's probably through crimes of upholstery – the cover-up will kill you.

– Joseph A. Grundfest

Professor of Law at Stanford University and
Former Commissioner of the Securities and Exchange Commission

In the lower corner of the tiny bit of newsprint was a happy face scrawled in green felt-tip ink.

"Oh man," Don chuckled as he left Jeffrey's office, "this is a day I'm glad not to be CEO."

Gloria contemplated calling Jeffrey to give him some advance warning about the sofa's arrival, but decided against it. She would rather not deal with his initial reaction by phone, especially if it included instructions to get rid of the thing before he returned. Monday would be here soon enough. Better to wait and let him see it for himself. She sighed loudly just imagining her boss's reaction. There would be no rush to send a thank you to Ed Easton – that was certain.

On Monday morning, the sight of the sofa stopped Jeffrey at the entrance to his office. His first reaction was a sputter of words and then he stared slack-jawed. He turned to Gloria for an explanation. She had been sitting at her desk holding her breath and looking busy. Smiling weakly she told him, "It's from Ed."

Jeffrey's sigh was audible. He turned on his heel and marched off. "Take care of that, Gloria," he said without looking her way as he walked past. "I'll be back after lunch."

In Jeffrey's morning absence, Gloria consulted with Jeffrey's wife, with Don Asher, and with the General Counsel's office. Then she contacted the in-house maintenance team and had the sofa moved to a far corner of Jeffrey's office. A courier package arrived at noon. In the box was a large cashmere throw in subtle tones that echoed those of the walls and furnishings in the executive suite. Gloria carefully draped the throw over two-thirds of the yellow sofa as shown in the diagram faxed to her from the interior designer in New York. One of the maintenance crew had already come and gone with a ladder to reposition the angle of two recessed lights, drawing attention away from the sofa's new location.

When Jeffrey returned after lunch he stopped in the doorway and leaned forward to peer around the corner into his office. Gloria watched carefully without actually staring. She was sure that for a brief moment Jeffrey thought the sofa was gone. And then he realized it wasn't.

"Alright then," Jeffrey mumbled, "if that's the best we can do."

"Yes. Everyone I consulted this morning about the sofa situation agreed. No matter how ugly the sofa is, it can't go into storage," Gloria explained. "It must stay in the CEO's office. It is, after all, a gift from Ed."

The Architect and the CEO

After the not-yet-famous architect designed The Easton Company's headquarters building, he went on to design a number of other unique properties for the company including the first entertainment mall in the United States. High-tech for the times, full of big screen theaters, interactive gaming, and futuristic shopping and dining options, it opened in California in the mid-'80s. Looking back, the architect liked to share with interviewers that it was during this "mall period" when he began privately designing more distinctive projects – the kind of signature structures that eventually made him famous. However, architect David Sinclair was still under contract to The Easton Company for a dozen more mundane but quite lucrative development projects. Projects that made pursuing his dreams seem impossibly out of reach.

When Andrew Heath, Easton's then-CEO, visited David Sinclair in his California studio, he got his first look at some of the dream projects the architect was designing on his own time. These were creations that far exceeded Easton's portfolio needs and Andrew recognized them as emerging works of genius. In a candid discussion over dinner and drinks that evening, Sinclair shared with Andrew the frustration of being legally bound to years of work he no longer wanted to do. Andrew Heath took pity on the man. The CEO told the architect to follow his calling. Then, with a handshake, Heath promised to release David Sinclair from his future contractual obligations to The Easton Company. Although Andrew Heath was a shrewd negotiator and had been Easton's chief legal counsel before becoming CEO, he clearly saw that there was little to be gained from a forced relationship with this budding architectural mastermind.

The CEO returned to the East Coast and advised his board of directors that the company would require a new architect. The appropriate papers were drawn up and executed, releasing David Sinclair from any further projects. At the time no one at Easton objected or voiced their disapproval. Sinclair had certainly been innovative, but he had also been a pain to work with. All the same ingredients that made the man a creative architect also made him unpredictable and unmanageable in a corporate environment with tight deadlines and restrictive budgets. Most senior staff members in Easton's development area were relieved to see him go…at least initially.

Several years later, after David Sinclair completed a bevy of amazing projects that vaulted him to international recognition, the grumblings at Easton began. Nearing retirement, Andrew Heath was branded as the executive who let the most famous architect since Frank Lloyd Wright get away. Heath was dumbfounded at this internal reaction. The same people who years before had endorsed the CEO's decision were now Monday morning quarterbacks on the severing of the Sinclair relationship, with musings about what might have been.

In an interview with *Architectural Digest*, David Sinclair was quoted saying Andrew Heath was responsible for "setting me free to become the architect I was born to be." But within The Easton Company Andrew Heath's record of accomplishments as CEO would always be tainted by being singularly responsible for terminating the relationship with David Sinclair.

Prior to his retirement, Andrew gave an interview to the Washington Post in which he reminisced about the wonderful projects he and the famous architect had worked on together, mentioning that the company owned nearly a dozen David Sinclair designed buildings including the Easton headquarters building. A short time later, the architect was in town for a dinner at the White House and happened to be interviewed by the same Post reporter who had interviewed Andrew Heath. So of course the reporter mentioned the structures Sinclair had designed for Easton in those early years, asking the architect what made them special.

"Oh those old things," Sinclair replied with his gap-toothed grin. "There is absolutely nothing special about them. They were done for cash, not from inspiration. During that same period I was designing gas stations and grocery stores."

Andrew Heath never quite lived that one down. One of his final acts as CEO was to remove the plaque in the lobby of The Easton Company headquarters that had proudly announced to visitors they were entering a David Sinclair building.

Despite David Sinclair's orphaning his Easton projects, the Easton headquarters building undeniably had one trait in common with many of the internationally recognized Sinclair masterworks – during heavy rains it leaked mercilessly.

50

Easton Transportation – Initial Approach

During the final years of The Easton Company, one subsidiary that flew under the radar was Easton Transportation, the legal entity that owned and operated the company's corporate jets. Until the plane crash that took the life of promising Easton executive Simon Miller, the company had used commercial airliners and chartered private planes to transport executives. But after the plane crash, everything changed. Risk managers took a long hard look at the company's insurance coverage versus Easton's corporate policy on executive business travel. All related issues went under the microscope.

At the close of this exhaustive study of travel policy and business practices, Jeffrey Elkins was named CEO. Influenced by his closet phobias, Jeffrey reviewed the study recommendations and decided he needed his own plane, flown by a pilot of his choosing who would be on the Easton payroll. Far beyond the study's findings on what was required for the good of the company, Jeffrey's decision was driven by a need for control. Thus Easton Transportation was established as a corporate subsidiary – a Learjet secured, a pilot, copilot and mechanic hired, and a hangar leased.

Executive Compensation – The Ripcord on the Golden Parachute

A rocket-surge in executive compensation and platinum parachute packages began near the end of the twentieth century. For those with an insider's eye, it was clear that the more CEOs asked for, the more they got; and the more they got, the more they wanted. As compensation director for The Easton Company, it was one emerging trend that infuriated T.J. Clarke.

Before joining Easton, Clarke worked as a compensation consultant in the Washington office of a national management consulting firm. The Easton Company was one of his top clients and they seemed to like T.J. as much as he enjoyed working on their account. T.J. was smart, soft spoken, and his appearance brought to mind a rugged young Sundance Kid in a suit and tie. Eventually, The Easton Company made T.J. an offer and hired him away from the consulting firm.

Larry Baxter, Easton's vice president of human resources, considered it a major coup when he managed to convince Clarke to join the company. Most of Easton's compensation management responsibilities had been piled on Larry's plate for years and he was thrilled with the prospect of delegating the analytical portion of compensation work to T.J. It was Larry Baxter's objective to have Clarke handle all the administrative compensation work while Larry continued as the primary compensation contact to senior management and the Easton board of directors. Once on board, however, it quickly became clear that T.J. Clarke knew a lot more about compensation management than his boss.

Larry Baxter had designed Easton's original compensation program and over the years held the thing together with sheer willpower. It was a complex hybrid of two very different standard compensation systems, with a heavy dose of Baxter's personal biases regarding relative job value thrown in. But the program had not kept pace with the times, which was one of the reasons T.J. Clarke was hired.

During his first year at The Easton Company, T.J. Clarke was considered a wonder boy. He advanced the company's compensation policies and procedures light-years by standardizing the use of market surveys. Then he introduced and implemented a new performance measurement system that was embraced by both supervisors and employees. The new annual review methodologies eliminated the veil of mystery employed by Larry Baxter to hide the shortcomings and subjective nature of the old evaluation process. At year-end, T.J. initiated a project to migrate the company's entire compensation process from paper and spreadsheet to a sophisticated software application.

Near the end of Clarke's first year at Easton, pressure was growing from one camp of senior managers to have T.J. assume some executive compensation responsibilities. Larry Baxter was not about to cede the power provided by his direct access to Easton's executive group, especially regarding executive compensation.

Concerned about his own job security, Larry decided to dampen management's enthusiasm for the new compensation director by spreading the word among his peers that T.J. wasn't up to the task. Over lunch or a cup of coffee, Larry began initiating conversations with other division heads on the subject of T.J. Clarke; about how he was a fantastic compensation analyst and great at managing the minutia and data, but when it came to possessing a progressive vision for the company's compensation program, he couldn't see the forest for the trees. Larry confided that T.J. was too wrapped up in the details to look up and see the big picture. Not exactly an ideal candidate for directing executive compensation.

At first, this line of conversation with the vice presidents was a tough sell. After all, T.J. Clarke had years of experience as a compensation consultant. How could he not have the vision necessary to handle executive compensation? Plus, T.J. was far more personable and charming than Larry Baxter. But Larry Baxter persisted, even hinting at concerns about confidentiality – a very serious charge in the world of executive pay – and noting by contrast his own years as a trusted advisor to senior management.

In his sole conversation on the topic with the CEO, Larry Baxter gave his pitch a different spin. Larry's argument to Jeffrey Elkins led Jeffrey to believe that, although T.J. Clarke might actually have some progressive ideas about new trends in compensation practices, it was Larry – not T.J. – who would always be loyal to the interests of the CEO, regardless of the latest developments in compensation programs and practices.

After Baxter left his office that day, Jeffrey Elkins chuckled to himself. Unbeknown to Larry Baxter, Jeffrey Elkins was quite comfortable having his VP of human resources continue as the company's compensation front man to the board and senior executives. Jeffrey had used Larry's shortcomings to convince the board to engage an executive compensation firm – professionals who could advise the company on CEO and top executive pay issues. Larry's mediocrity allowed Jeffrey to continue using the Manhattan-based consultant who masterminded Jeffrey's recent executive retention agreement. Thomas Williams & Co. was one of the leading executive compensation firms in the country, and Elkins wasn't about to let some middle manager muddy the waters with grand ideas about company-wide compensation reform.

In Jeffrey's opinion, executive compensation was a world apart from compensation management for the rank and file. He wanted nothing disrupting the relationship Easton had established with Thomas Williams & Co. They clearly understood compensation design for the CEO class.

Easton Transportation – The Plane, The Plane!

In the beginning the corporate jet was for the exclusive use of Easton's CEO and any invited executives or guests traveling with him on company business. For a full year only Easton's board of directors, the risk management director, and a handful of senior employees were aware that the company was no longer chartering planes but had purchased one. Its existence finally surfaced as the focus of an internal audit report including a cost/benefit analysis of corporate jet ownership compared to chartering, leasing, and flying commercial airlines. The report demonstrated that it would be more cost efficient for the company to return to chartering jets for the CEO, given his exclusive use of this transportation and the number of hours the plane and pilot were spending on the ground. As the report was reviewed by a number of company accountants, Easton's plane was now "out of the hangar."

Jeffrey Elkins was not happy. He called the audit director to his office to have him personally present the recommendation.

Mark Dixon, the corporate audit director, was a nervous person under the best of circumstances. He found it difficult to sit still during meetings and often wandered around a room picking up and replacing objects as he talked. Dixon knew that if you were lowlier than a vice president, a summons to the CEO's office was never good news. Mr. Elkins' secretary did not call to schedule an appointment; instead she told Mark to be in the CEO's office in ten minutes to discuss the internal audit report on corporate jet usage. The sweating began the moment he hung up the phone. Now sitting face to face with Jeffrey Elkins in the CEO's office to explain his recommendation was causing Dixon to perspire heavily from the neck up. He felt like a human fountain.

After listening to Dixon nervously read the recommendation from his audit report, Jeffrey Elkins shot him a mildly disgusted look and then stood up and stretched.

"That's all well and good," Elkins began "but what you're failing to report is how else we might fix this."

Now Dixon was really getting nervous. What exactly did Elkins have in mind? His brain went to all the wrong places as he tried to come up with some sort of acceptable business response. Dixon's heart was pounding. He was barely able to control his nervous urge to reach out and touch the stuff on the CEO's desk.

"Fix this?" he repeated. "How do you mean, sir?" It was taking all his concentration not to pick up the Baccarat crystal paperweight sitting within arm's reach. Dixon closed his eyes to escape the temptation.

Jeffrey started walking around his office, looking out the expanse of windows facing the lake. Dixon wanted badly to get up from his chair and move around too, but he knew better.

"Well, Mark, you've told me that current usage of the assets doesn't justify ownership. So my question to you is, what's the alternative? Other than sell the plane, I mean."

Dixon's mind was stuck. It was taking all his mental powers to keep his nervous habits in check. He wasn't following wherever the CEO was going with this. All he could think to say was, "You want me to change the report?" which came out of his mouth as a hoarse squeaky whisper.

Still looking out the window, Jeffrey rolled his eyes and made a mental note to help this guy find the exit door at some appropriate future point in time.

"No, Mark. What I'm saying is, what kind of usage numbers would justify keeping the plane? If we expanded the availability to other senior executives for business travel, where's the threshold for making this cost effective."

"Oh." Mark replied, feeling like an idiot. "I suppose we can take a look at that." The auditor's hand darted forward and his fingers briefly brushed one of the cold sharp facets of the paperweight, then quickly recoiled as the CEO began speaking again.

"Do me a favor, Mark. Don't just look at it. Study it. Then get back to me with the metrics. Then we'll come up with a new recommendation and draft the appropriate executive travel policies."

"Anything else?" Mark stammered. As Elkins turned to face him, Mark realized that under the circumstances, this was not a good question to ask the CEO.

"Yeah, Mark. Next time, don't make me do your job for you."

The auditor's face turned bright red as he quickly stood to leave. His hands were shaking and his legs felt like gelatin. Even before he made it to the door, he knew there would be no "next time." In a corporate environment where there were no second chances, it was the first and last visit Mark Dixon ever made to Jeffrey Elkins' office.

As a result of the revised audit report, the policy on corporate jet usage was extended to the five most senior executives. Easton was expanding, building new developments and acquiring new properties all around the country. It would be no problem for the cross-country traveling executives to meet the usage requirements outlined in the revised audit.

It was not long, however, before a new problematic issue developed. Jeffrey no longer had control of his plane. Conflicting schedules and flight requests to different locations meant Jeffrey often had to make his execs unhappy, bumping them from using the jet whenever he needed it. He felt like he was sharing a car with kid brothers.

Along with scheduling issues, Jeffrey's personal health concerns and hygiene phobias were exacerbated by the new arrangements. It was one thing to fly with other people of his choosing and observe what they did. It was quite another to have other people use his plane without him. His imagination about onboard activities was unrestrained.

In Jeffrey's defense, there were times when his imagination intersected with reality. With more frequent use of the plane by members of the senior executive group – five very different individuals with an assortment of personal lives and personalities – some choice stories began to leak out. A few became material for Easton company lore.

One favorite tale involved an executive who sent the company jet to pick up his son from college at the end of term. Onboard were two members of Easton's building maintenance staff. The two employees weren't exactly sure why they were dispatched until they arrived at the kid's dorm and realized they were there to pack and move all his stuff. When the two employees returned to the airport with a station wagon crammed full of dorm room furnishings, the pilot flipped out. There was no way all that college student junk was going on his plane – not while he was Easton's pilot. In the end, one employee flew home with the executive's son and a few of his choice belongings while the other employee drove eleven hours back to Virginia with the remainder of the kid's possessions.

Eventually, the travel demands of the senior group would justify the purchase of a second jet. But this new corporate jet would be Jeffrey's alone. The rest of them could share the existing Learjet. He would have his own.

The company jet story that remained dearest to most employees, however, occurred late in the life of The Easton Company. The year before the merger, a long-service mailroom employee reached his forty-fifth anniversary with the company. At age nineteen, the man has started out as Ed Easton's driver. No other employee had ever achieved the forty-five-year milestone, and at the annual company-wide anniversary function, Jeffrey Elkins personally presented the specially made forty-five-year anniversary pin to Morris Smith.

Beginning at twenty-five years of service, Easton employees celebrating milestone anniversaries were provided a rather significant gift of their own choosing – a leather jacket, a stone garden bench, a bracelet from Tiffany & Co. But on the day of the anniversary presentations, Morris still hadn't chosen a gift. Basking in the post-presentation ambiance of the amassed corporate employees, Jeffrey was feeling more social than usual. Knowing that Morris had not yet selected a gift, Elkins asked Morris what he might choose to commemorate forty-five years with the company. Morris looked down at his own feet. He rubbed his large rough hands one on top of the other, then reached up and rubbed the back of his neck, rocking nervously from side to side.

"Um, well, um, Mr. Jeffrey," the big sixty-four-year-old man began, "I haven't ever been to Vegas…" at which point his voice trailed off and a string of "um"s and "uh"s began again.

"I see," Elkins responded. But still Morris Smith was looking at his shoes. "Well…"

"Um…and I haven't ever ridden in the corporate plane neither!" Morris finally finished in one exhaled rush.

"Oh. My…" Jeffrey reacted by taking a short step back as Morris finally raised his sad, smiling eyes to look Jeffrey Elkins directly in the face. Elkins quickly realized two of Smith's friends from the mailroom were standing close enough to hear this conversation, and they were smiling, trying not to laugh.

"Well, Morris," Jeffrey recovered, "we'll have to see what we can do." And with that Jeffrey Elkins spun around and headed for an exit.

Jeffrey hoped Morris would never have the nerve to follow up on his request, but word got out among employees, and eventually – to save face and be done with the ordeal – he agreed to send Morris and his wife (the man actually had the nerve to assume the gift included his wife) for a weekend in Las Vegas with transportation provided on the company jet. To add legitimacy to the travel, arrangements were made for Morris Smith to tour Easton's development facilities in Vegas, but it was all so transparent.

"He's a mailroom clerk, for God's sake!" Elkins had erupted when he was informed about the tour.

Although the trip to Vegas for the mail clerk took place long before the SEC and the IRS issued tougher rules distinguishing what makes a trip personal and not business, just the idea of it made Jeffrey nervous. He dragged his feet on approving Morris Smith's anniversary trip for several months, but in the end he let it happen. Morris Smith and his wife flew to Las Vegas two weeks before Jeffrey's new "CEO only" corporate jet was delivered. After Morris returned from Vegas, Elkins never boarded the Learjet again.

Jeffrey's new corporate jet was a Hawker 800A. Jeffrey had it customized for his height, allowing him to stand erect in the plane without hunching, as the Learjet required. The Hawker had been built to his and his pilot's specifications and customized with the best avionics. He designed the configuration of the six chairs with optional divan seating and he even selected the interior color pallet. By the time the Hawker was delivered, it boasted a long list of high end installations including: Video Airshow 400, a Grimes Pulselite System, a Safe Flight Windshear Detection System, Devore Tel-Tail lights, an Avalon Acoustics CD sound system, and Jura coffee machine.

The Hawker was Jeffrey's joy – it made him feel happy in ways he hadn't experienced in quite a while. With his new plane and his trusted personal pilot, it was once again a pleasure to fly.

Annual Review

One of the duties Jeffrey Elkins delegated to Larry Baxter was to meet with the CEO's pilot and present his annual performance review. Larry disliked this responsibility for a number of reasons – primarily because the pilot worked exclusively for Jeffrey Elkins. The only time Larry ever saw the pilot was when annual review time rolled around. Each year Jeffrey wrote up a short narrative paragraph of praise and gave it to Larry along with the pilot's raise and bonus numbers. The CEO expected Larry to convert that information into a formal performance document and then meet with the pilot to deliver the review. Larry felt awkward imparting secondhand information as the pilot grinned and nodded from across the room.

Jake Martin, CMDR USN Ret., didn't do much to make Larry feel at ease. Martin always arrived precisely on time at Larry's office dressed in his well-tailored pilot's uniform, his brimmed hat tucked securely under one arm, black shoes shined to a high gloss. Jake Martin consistently greeted Larry Baxter with his outstretched, unnaturally tanned hand and artificially white-toothed smile. The pilot's very presence triggered feelings of inferiority and insecurity in Larry that had been suppressed since junior high school.

Jake Martin was Jeffery Elkins' first choice for corporate pilot. One interview made the CEO feel secure and safe – and they weren't even in the air. The retired Navy man exuded calm confidence without a hint of ego. Jake Martin was an exceptional pilot and he knew it – there was no need to brag or boost his resume. What he wanted from an employer was trust and respect.

His personal story was interesting but largely irrelevant to his qualifications. Born and raised in Florida, at age eighteen he applied to and was accepted at the Naval Academy. He loved everything about Annapolis and made the most of his four years there. Jake knew he wanted to fly and after flight school his desire quickly landed him in Vietnam near the end of the war. His extended tour of duty kept him in the service through the departure of American forces in 1975. He flew evacuations from the American Embassy that year, and later was stationed in Thailand as the U.S. government's attentions turned to Laos. During the most stressful periods of his duty, Jake Martin found solace and sanity in his dreams of returning to the charms of the Annapolis area with its four distinct seasons and the beauty of the Chesapeake Bay.

After his early retirement from the Navy, he bounced around for a brief period, looking for an opportunity that felt right. Then came a call from a Navy buddy who had recently gone to work for Federal Express.

"They're recruiting pilots, Jake. The money's good and it's a solid company to work for. You should come to Tennessee and check it out."

Flying for FedEx felt effortless after the war. It was a great gig in the companionship of pleasant and reasonable people who respected and rewarded hard work and excellent skills. But after a few years Jake got restless. Tennessee was okay, but he missed being near the water. He started scanning ads for private pilots in trade magazines. Not just any pilot job, Jake was looking for something specific. It took nearly eighteen months, but one evening as he paged through Aviation Week, there it was: an ad for a full-time corporate pilot in the greater Washington, D.C. area.

Now, what seemed like a lifetime later, Jake Martin was happily working for Easton Transportation. At forty-eight, he looked every bit the part of a corporate pilot, just as his boss had the classic appearance of an American CEO. When they exited the plane together, they could draw stares – in part due to their good looks and chiseled features, but also because their heights differed by nearly a foot. Jake was short, tan, and trim with dark eyes and dark hair graying slightly at the temples. He loved the corporate pilot lifestyle. He lived in a stunning home on the Severn River near Annapolis and flew regularly to Vegas, San Diego, Miami, Austin and occasionally London. He enjoyed piloting a corporate jet for a CEO who sincerely appreciated his abilities. Best of all, his job description was blissfully simple: fly the plane and keep one person happy – Jeffrey Elkins.

Comp Gap 101

When word traveled back to T.J. Clarke about the rumors Larry Baxter was spreading concerning his competencies, T.J. was furious. For weeks afterward, he sat behind his closed office door and brooded on what to do. He even discussed the situation with several of his closest colleagues, including his long-time mentor at the consulting firm he previously worked for in Washington. In these conversations, T.J. played out his "what if" fantasies of confronting Larry Baxter, or scheduling a private meeting with the CEO to enlighten him about T.J.'s compensation knowledge relative to that of his boss. He even considered stirring up a confrontation between Larry and some of the division heads who continued to be impressed with T.J.'s skills despite Larry Baxter's insults.

Ultimately, T.J. did none of these things. Some informed observers surmised that T.J.'s inaction resulted from his hatred of confrontation. He couldn't bear to initiate one. Others thought it was his distaste for any change to his established daily routine and habits, and a major confrontation would likely result in a job search and a new employer.

Although both observations about T.J.'s personality were accurate, the main reason he chose to do nothing about Larry Baxter's assault on his abilities was the realization that, in the end, he would gain nothing and risk losing everything. More than confrontations and change, T.J. Clarke hated to lose.

Instead, T.J. decided to remain at Easton and quietly champion fair compensation practices for the average employee. Although he acknowledged his efforts were quixotic, T.J. still considered it a noble cause. To do this, he would need to stay on top of every relevant salary survey available. He would also have to closely follow all the established and emerging executive compensation trends in the industry. Larry Baxter would need to keep up if he wanted to continue discrediting T.J. as a dim bulb.

The more T.J. Clarke studied the developments in the gap between executive compensation and everyman's pay, the more disgruntled he became. In the two years between Clarke's fall from wonder boy status and the day The Easton Company was sold, there was plenty to be angry about.

The phenomenon of creating lottery-size pay increases for top executives was helped along by the innovations of the nation's leading executive compensation consultants, who were profiting wildly from their advice. It would be a few more years after the sale of The Easton Company, and multibillion dollars more in U.S. mergers and acquisitions, before the IRS began playing hardball on executive compensation. It would take even longer for Congress to start asking questions and taking names to determine whether all this expensive consulting advice regarding executive compensation was truly independent.

Meanwhile, reload stock options – the financial equivalent of a perpetual motion money machine – helped give millions of valuable stock shares to executives, until a change to the accounting rules unplugged the machine. A compensation consultant had invented reloads, too.

But little changed despite all the fierce talk about reining in executive compensation practices after Enron, Tyco, and a slew of other big payouts and bad press credited to top corporate executives. In fact, negotiated CEO pay packages just kept getting bigger. Sure there were a few CEOs – Steve Jobs and Ben and Jerry for example – who were attempting to do the right thing by capping their cash compensation or taking only one dollar in annual salary in answer to the universal questions: When is enough really enough? How much can one person deservedly earn? What should be the maximum x-factor when comparing CEO compensation to the pay of an employee in the lowest job within the same organization?

For T.J. Clarke and many other observers of the executive comp phenomenon, it all boiled down to one searing ethical issue: How can an organization justify giving rank-and-file employees four percent raises for excellent performance when the CEO could sink the ship – or better yet, sell it out from under himself – and walk away with a king's ransom?

PART THREE

LEADING UP TO ANNOUNCEMENT DAY

Thought Leader

In the months immediately preceding the announcement of the sale of The Easton Company, T.J. Clarke closely followed the widening gap between executive compensation and everyman compensation within the company. The company initiated several rounds of layoffs and opened an early retirement window accompanied by a modest incentive package targeted at long-service administrative employees. It was clear to T.J. that the company was attempting to get lean to make itself more attractive. But attractive to whom? Stockholders? Lending institutions? Potential buyers? T.J. considered each of these possibilities.

Then came the hiring of Lee Martino as Easton's chief operating officer, and the swift early retirement of three senior company executives, each of whom had been perceived as a potential successor to the CEO if Jeffrey Elkins ever retired. All three had spent their careers at Easton and were serious businessmen. To the surprise of most corporate employees, each had walked out the door with a big package and the sure knowledge that they would not be the next CEO of The Easton Company.

Around the time Lee Martino joined the company, T.J. Clarke began quietly sharing with friends his vision of what was coming: the sale of The Easton Company. T.J. continued to repeat his theory whenever conversation among coworkers turned to recent company decisions that somehow failed to fit the history and framework of Easton's corporate culture. The reaction from his fellow employees was outright disbelief when he predicted in a low voice, "They're going to sell the company – I just know it."

Long-service employees who couldn't begin to imagine a world without The Easton Company would always quickly disagree.

"Oh T.J.," they would say, "you're such a pessimist. That's not going to happen."

T.J.'s response was always the same. With a look of brooding disappointment on his face, he'd silently return to his office and shut the door, totally convinced – despite his workmates' reactions – that he was the prophet of doom and the day of reckoning was near.

Three months before news of the company's sale hit the airwaves, T.J. Clarke was invited to speak at a regional compensation and benefits symposium on the topic of executive compensation trends. He accepted gladly, knowing the invitation was made based on the reputation of his employer more than his own. Larry Baxter tried but failed to intervene after hearing from a colleague that T.J. was on the speaker's list. T.J.'s former boss at the consulting firm had suggested the speaking invitation to the July symposium, and the firm was one of the event's sponsors.

T.J. Clarke's executive compensation presentation featured the level of detail many expected. There were plenty of charts, graphs and statistics that reflected his love of the topic's fine points. Then T.J. stunned the room with his summarizing comments:

"The persistent problem we face in executive compensation at the beginning of the twenty-first century is lack of transparency. From a reasonable person's perspective, there is no sound logical explanation for the value given to a CEO's job in relationship to the pay of everyone else in a company – no matter how hard we attempt to spin it."

T.J. could sense his audience audibly holding their collective breath. This was not the message they were expecting at a business leaders compensation and benefits symposium.

"These huge paydays for executives are a major contributor to the perception – and in some cases the reality – of the gap between the very wealthy and everyone else in the American workplace. Let's be honest. Exactly what is it that these gentlemen are doing to make their contribution worth so very much more than all the other workers in the same organization? When the CEO's base pay is $4.35 million, how much should the receptionist be making?"

Looking out into his audience, T.J. saw what was always obvious in any gathering of human resources professionals – significantly more females in the room than males.

"And yes, we're definitely talking about men. If you want to know how women executives are making out in the world of executive compensation compared to their male peers, flip through the pages of any merger Schedule 14-D and look for women among the list of Named Executive Officers who are getting special treatment in these deals. If you find one, make sure to notice that, no matter their titles or credentials, even in the world of merger bonanzas, the women are getting significantly less than the men."

Pausing briefly T.J. took a slow, deep breath as he headed for the conclusion of his speech.

"The concept of market driven CEO pay may be one of the biggest hoaxes in corporate America. It's pure fiction that top executive pay packages are constructed by independent compensation consultants. Clearly, when the same consulting house is hired for additional projects and services, it becomes difficult to recommend executive pay restraints that might jeopardize their other business with the same client, thus stifling any hope for independent guidance.

"What about the role of a company's board of directors in these situations? Unfortunately, the compensation committee of a board is often no better than the proverbial fox watching over the hen house. Commonly, directors who demonstrate the slightest concern about executive pay excesses mysteriously never make it to, or are promptly bounced from, the board's compensation committee.

"And what about the role of government? No matter the level of interest and intervention by Congress, the courts, or the SEC in the area of executive compensation, it will take a lot to convince me that executive compensation decisions are given the same scrutiny as other business decisions in any for-profit corporation.

"I have to agree with that business writer in the *Washington Post* – Steven Pearlstein – who wrote: 'We'll know there's a true free market evaluation of executive comp taking place when an executive comp firm by the name of Hard Bargain Associates shows up to claim the best track record for securing from skilled CEOs the highest level of performance for the least amount of money.'"

As T.J. stepped away from the dais to a combination of polite and enthusiastic applause, one of the other presenters – a silver-haired gentleman in a very expensive suit – leaned over and whispered into T.J.'s ear, "Who the hell do you think you are?"

Turning to face the man who was pretending to clap and smile for the benefit of the audience, T.J. firmly replied, "Oh, I know who I am. I'm T.J. Clarke, your new creative thought leader on matters involving everyman compensation."

What Happens In Vegas…

On a hot day in late May Jeffrey Elkins casually stopped George Miles in the corridor outside the annual real estate developers conference and asked if he had dinner plans.

Elkins had speculated about this encounter for months before it actually happened. Inviting the head of your major competitor to dinner certainly wasn't a common occurrence, even during these annual industry events. For too long now he'd been thinking about the possibilities – and the outcome.

Six months earlier Elkins first planted the seed of change with his senior executives during a company meeting also held in Las Vegas. He'd explained where The Easton Company fell in the pecking order of its competitors and spelled out the current realities of this dog-eat-dog business. As of the previous spring, all their remaining U.S. competitors were family owned and controlled. The Easton Company was not. It was only a matter of time before a hostile takeover or a white knight situation might present itself.

His executives listened attentively, asked a few polite questions, talked among themselves, and then intellectually set aside the CEO's comments during the plane ride home. Their perspective focused on a different set of factors. Among its peers, The Easton Company was an industry leader with a respectable history and deep roots in the community. The corporation was profitable, viable, and stable. A takeover of any sort seemed inconceivable.

Jeffrey pondered his executives' reaction. They're all too comfortable, he thought. I won't speak of it again until after I've floated the idea of a sale to a potential buyer. Then I'll know more about the possibilities.

Over a bottle of Opus One Meritage and grain fed, free range bison filets, Jeffrey Elkins made George Miles' eyes light up. Pratt-Miles was about the same size as The Easton Company, but its properties were definitely more middle class, while Easton was known for its diamond-level developments.

70

By the tilt of George Miles' head, Jeffrey knew he was already mentally running the numbers. Pratt-Miles was cash rich and had a reputation for "buying up" in the world of mergers and acquisitions. Buying The Easton Company would be a very big deal – the biggest in Pratt-Miles history. It would not be easy but it would be lucrative.

Just like in the game of Monopoly, when you have a handful of Illinois Avenue and someone offers you a chance to buy a fistful of Park Place, mouths water. Game on. Roll the dice. Let the negotiations begin.

Get On Board

"What in the world is going on?" Turning the corner into summer, that question started nearly every closed-door session among the Easton employment staff. Their impromptu meetings characterized by intense whispers and occasional expletives had been ongoing for nearly a week. The situation at hand was peculiar for The Easton Company. In the midst of an unusual downsizing program at corporate headquarters affecting administrative staff and support personnel, here they were suddenly interviewing for three newly created executive positions. These high level jobs were not in the budget, nor on anyone's wish list for the current fiscal year. It was a puzzle. There were a number of hunches, but no one could figure it out.

The employment staff had just completed a series of meetings with administrative employees affected by the downsizing. They were primarily older women with long service whose jobs were being eliminated. The one-on-one appointments were painful and the employment department had exhausted boxes of tissues as tears flowed. The enhanced pension benefits and severance payments were generous for the industry and the region, but very few of the targeted employees wanted to leave The Easton Company. That was always the problem. Hardly anyone ever chose to leave unless they were moving, retiring or dead.

The downsizing had made it a rough month and it reflected the mood of the headquarters staff. The soon-to-depart employees were quite popular and well known to their fellow workers. Many were female employees who had been instrumental in carrying on Easton company traditions, giving their time and talents to mark holidays, birthdays and other important occasions. Some were part of Easton's informal social committee; the group that always volunteered to help run the company's charity events, fundraisers, and

72

celebratory luncheons. Newer corporate employees quietly speculated that was one reason these individuals' jobs were being eliminated. As employees in a fast-paced, demanding Fortune 500 corporation, the social committee group seemed to have too much work time available for so much social frivolity. Employees who had been around longer saw it differently. They sensed the company was eliminating these jobs to get rid of the people who fostered the Easton culture from an earlier era.

The employment staff was seasoned enough to know that layoffs were never easy. Sometimes, however, it was a necessary process organizations had to endure to reach the next level of performance.

What was causing the closed doors and whispered discussions in human resources wasn't about the twenty-three administrative jobs being eliminated. The layoff program was part of the company's less publicized annual goals to decrease payroll costs at headquarters – something investment analysts had been criticizing Easton for during the past year. The mystery was the sudden addition of the three executive positions to headquarters staff with instructions from the most senior levels to fill the jobs immediately.

No sooner had the HR recruiters developed the sketchiest of job descriptions for the new positions than the employment manager received a call from the vice president of marketing. He was sending over a resume for a "prime candidate" for one of the two new director level positions on his staff.

"Please set up an interview with this person as soon as possible. I've already talked with him. I've worked with him in the past and he's good. He's who I want. So let's not waste any time getting him on board."

Generally this wasn't how hiring a six-figure executive went down at The Easton Company. There were protocols, processes and various checks to go through. Now the employment staff was getting the hurry-up by the hiring executive to fill a new position with a pre-selected colleague. Not good.

Then it got worse. Within two days the same scenario had played out with the other two new positions. Another call from the marketing VP, another resume, and clear direction that no further search was necessary. The vice president of development was more direct.

"Hire the guy I'm sending you. I'll send over his resume but the interview is just pro forma."

The directness of instruction to hire without a proper search process made the employment staff infuriated and uneasy. Given the power and position of the hiring executives, the lowly Easton recruiting staff fumed, but followed directions. After interviewing both candidates for the two marketing positions, the recruiters met offsite to compare notes in a quiet corner booth at a local Chinese restaurant.

"I can't believe we're hiring these guys. They're both first class idiots," Sean began in a loud stage whisper.

"The first one was a real flamer with the kind of ego we normally avoid like the plague, unless they're a rainmaker, and there's absolutely no evidence of that. The second one didn't even begin to meet our director level qualifications," Terry added. "And I wouldn't be surprised to learn his resume is full of faux credentials."

"He's definitely not director material."

"Do you think the second candidate will pass the drug test?"

"Are we really going to pay these losers $116,500 base pay?"

"Since when do we suddenly need a restaurant marketing director and a hotel marketing director? Are we getting into developing restaurants and hotels now?"

"And what about those signing bonuses and the rest of their lucrative packages?" Terry hissed. "Since when are we enriching the packages more than twenty percent?"

"What I'd like to know is how will we justify these hires on the heels of the layoffs. The most any one of those admins was making was $38,200. It's gonna look bad no matter how it gets dressed up by management."

"So Terry – what did Larry have to say when you asked him if we were really hiring these guys?"

"He was super grumpy but he said yes, we were hiring them ASAP. Period. Then he told me to stop asking questions and that we should all stop chattering about it. Just pull up our big kid pants and get on with it."

"I think this is the year we're sinking to a new low. If they want to hire whomever they want, what the hell do they need us for?" Sean seethed.

"Check please," Terry said to the waitress passing their booth. "Time to pull up our big kid pants and get back to work."

After completing their new hire paperwork and benefits enrollment materials, the three new executives were never seen again in the headquarters offices. They didn't even show for mandatory orientation. Excuses were made – they were already on the road doing their jobs – but the employment staff remained suspicious.

Health Care Country Club

SUMMIT EXECUTIVE CARE
PRIVILEGED AND TRUSTED ACCESS TO THE HIGHEST QUALITY
HEALTH CARE IN THE WORLD

As a senior executive for a Fortune 500 company, the last place you ever want to be is in a hospital emergency room. Your time, your health and your life are too valuable to be left to chance. Confronted with a health issue – large or small – you and your family deserve the best care available, no matter where it's provided or when, or how. You need access to the very best medicine delivered by the top one percent of medical professionals in the world. Your lifestyle demands nothing less. That's why you need Summit Executive Care. Your lifetime membership awaits.

Flipping through the exquisite brochure one more time after reading that paragraph, Jeffrey Elkins sighed and felt his face relax into a slight smile. Spending time looking at the Summit Executive Care literature stirred in him the same euphoric feeling as studying the newest Mercedes catalog or a Relais et Chateau destinations booklet. He wanted this. He needed this. No, he deserved this.

Here was a company that had figured out how to get the best health care into the hands of those who most deserved it – important, top-tier executives like him. People who didn't have time to waste on anything less than the very best health care delivered in the best settings by the more experienced hands and minds in their fields. And all of it available with immediate and unlimited access – anywhere, any time.

The brochure explained that in serious situations, Summit Executive Care members were transported for services by medical helicopter, private medical jet, or ambulance limousine. For doctor's appointments, Summit provided transportation by chauffeured town car for local care or by private jet or first class air travel, depending on the distance.

A dedicated personal health care advisor, serving as both liaison and care coordinator, was assigned to each member. The advisor's duties included accompanying the member to appointments and services, keeping track of necessary medical records, providing the member with comprehensive progressive medical intelligence, and securing and delivering prescriptions and medicines to the member's home or office. Each member's personal advisor was the 24/7 conduit to all the fine services Summit provided and assured access and continuity of care without the member's involvement – other than supplying oneself for the actual appointments, tests and procedures. No more waiting rooms, insurance forms, or health questionnaires. Advisors even filled the role of communicating with other designated family members about health care situations. One member was quoted saying that having his advisor was like having his own health care employee. It all added up to the ideal health care experience.

"How much is it worth to have someone you trust take care of all your health care needs, enabling you to focus on other matters?" the brochure posed. Both individual executive memberships and family memberships were available. There was a one-time initiation fee and then an annual membership payment. There were two levels of membership – diamond and platinum – with significantly different initiation fees. The platinum level was a lifetime membership, which was highly encouraged, since membership availability was limited not just by ability to pay but also by a set of status criteria. Summit was definitely interested in knowing and serving an established, exclusive membership base. It reminded Jeffrey of his Augusta National Golf Club membership, only this Summit membership was even more elite.

The fees seemed reasonable to Jeffrey. After all, what was the true value of a CEO's good health? With this type of arrangement, top executives could remain undistracted knowing their own care and the health care of their family members was being provided by the industry's best. It was well worth the fees to eliminate the worry and distraction.

Why hadn't someone thought of this concept long ago, Jeffrey wondered. The quarter million dollar initiation fee was a no-brainer as far as he was concerned. It would be money well spent. Not to mention just in time. Actually, time was the only factor Jeffrey was concerned about regarding the Summit arrangement: How to add it to his executive employment agreement in a timely manner and have it all in place before selling the company. Executing it might require offering the benefit to a few members of the change in control group who met Summit's personal membership criteria –

and only some of them would make the grade. The key would be to assure the memberships were secured, fees paid and paperwork completed in time for the Summit membership to be included in the change in control documents. The specifics of Summit's benefits would need to be carefully couched for stockholder consumption, but that could be handled when the time came. He'd leave the details for others to sort out.

Jeffrey penned a quick note on his personal company memo stationary that simply read:

June 23

Larry —

How quickly can we get this in place? Make it happen. Pronto.

Jeffrey

Jeffrey attached his note to the brochure. He also included the Summit representative's business card with the embossed gold lettering that had been given to him by one of his golfing compatriots. How very timely, Jeffrey thought once again.

"Gloria," he called quietly. His secretary sat immediately outside his door.

"Yes, Mr. Elkins?" Gloria replied as she promptly appeared in his doorway.

"Drop this in one of my For Immediate Attention envelopes and have it delivered directly into Larry Baxter's hands as soon as possible."

Medicine Man

Larry Baxter shook his head and sighed audibly when he opened the maroon envelope. It was marked CONFIDENTIAL – FOR IMMEDIATE ATTENTION and displayed Jeffery Elkins' monogram in the upper left hand corner. How redundant, Larry thought. Who in their right mind would not give their immediate attention to anything sent to them by the CEO? Now here was one more project added to the stack of new human resources initiatives related to the merger that required his immediate attention.

With the merger news yet to be announced, everything in the stack was solely Larry's responsibility. He could not delegate any of it to his extensive staff as long as the negotiations remained undisclosed. It made him frustrated, anxious and angry all at once. The key was to hold it together just a few weeks longer and give Jeffery everything he was asking for, with hopes of being rewarded with a richer change in control package. The challenge was that much of what Jeffrey was requesting required detailed knowledge beyond Larry's expertise. If he could only pass some of these projects off to the appropriate staff members, the work would get done in no time. But that wasn't going to happen.

Flipping through the brochure Jeffrey had sent from Summit Executive Care, it almost seemed like a bad joke. Larry had recently reminded the CEO about the need to address the future of Easton's retiree medical benefits in the ongoing negotiations with Pratt-Miles. Easton provided retiree medical and Pratt-Miles didn't. Jeffrey's reaction had been dismissive.

"Matters like that can sink a deal if disclosed too early. I'll raise the issue when the time is right," Elkins had indignantly responded.

Now Jeffrey was looking to secure his own health care benefits for life. However, maybe this was a good thing, Larry mused. It could be a sign that Jeffrey wasn't forgetting about the retiree medical benefits. Time would tell.

As Larry turned to the pricing sheet included at the back of the brochure, his mouth fell open.

"Good Lord," he said out loud. How could Jeffrey justify spending this kind of money to secure high-end health care benefits for an elite few while leaving the fate of the retirees' health care plan in jeopardy? Larry could feel his blood pressure rising. He took three slow deep breaths and looked out his window at the tree line. OK, he thought, maybe securing this executive health plan for the top tier will make guaranteeing the existing retiree medical benefits an easier sell. Certainly the actuarial cost for the entire Easton retiree population would be less than the cost of this executive medical plan for a dozen or fewer senior employees. Maybe this was part of Jeffrey's strategy. Larry could hope so anyway. He certainly wasn't about to call the CEO to initiate a discussion about it. The note had said, "Make it happen. Pronto." Not "Call if you would like to pick my brain about what the hell I'm thinking."

Larry got up and shut his office door, then returned to his chair and picked up the gold embossed business card from the Summit marketing representative. Looking at the card and at Jeffrey's hand written instructional note, he muttered, "It's not like I have a choice in the matter." Larry sighed again, reached for his phone and dialed the number on the card. "Hello Trevor? Larry Baxter here from The Easton Company. I'm calling on behalf of our CEO Jeffrey Elkins."

Security Matters – Monday Before the Announcement

It was a rough week for Brad Mather in the hot days of August just before the merger announcement. Brad was Easton's corporate director of property management. He negotiated and managed the regional service contracts for the malls that the company developed and still owned. Within the property management profession, his was a plum assignment. Brad's job focused primarily on the macro issues related to third party contracts for property maintenance, landscaping, heating/air-conditioning, and security. These functions were much more attractive from a plush office at corporate headquarters than they were up close onsite. Brad had done his time in the world of single property management and he was certainly glad those days were over. Better to contract out property services and leave personnel issues to the contractors.

Unfortunately, The Easton Company still maintained a few smaller properties in parts of the country where it was difficult to contract security services. When security personnel problems arose at those facilities, the property managers came to Brad. He could usually resolve most issues without consulting Easton's corporate human resources or legal staff. Brad had a wealth of expertise to draw from – enough that he often joked he could fill a book with his stories about the adventures and escapades of his property management days.

One such Easton property was a modest-sized shopping mall located in a middle-income Midwest suburb. This was an older mall with less prestigious anchor stores and fewer national chains than the big city malls. However, with limited other shopping options available in the area, this mall remained the community hub, maintained fairly good sales numbers, and it was fully leased. The primary reason the property was still in Easton's portfolio related to its history. It was one of the first properties Easton developed outside the

Washington area, and it had been one of the first enclosed malls in the American heartland. But these days, this mall was more a pain in Brad Mather's side than anything else. It certainly didn't add value to the cache of high-end diamond level properties that comprised the bulk of The Easton Company's assets.

Long before 9/11, U.S. shopping malls were already experiencing their share of security challenges. Security staff often consisted of younger police academy dropouts and older local law enforcement retirees – cop wannabes and cop retirees. The two groups brought different strengths and weaknesses to mall security.

Hiring the right people to provide dependable security staffing was a perpetual struggle. The picture of mall security had been the same for years, and it was the property manager's job to effectively utilize the staff available to handle the ebb and flow of crowd control throughout the day.

This Easton mall ran three 8-hour security shifts. The morning shift assignments were coveted jobs. First shift arrived a few minutes before 7 a.m., just in time to relieve the bleary-eyed night shift. After conducting their first rounds and completing a bit of paperwork it was time to open the merchant entrance doors. An hour later, the main doors were unlocked by security to accommodate access to the coffee shops and admit the mall walkers. Especially in colder months, the mall let locals use the enclosed shopping area as a morning exercise walking track. At that hour the mall attracted mostly retirees, and if they stayed around after walking to buy a cup of coffee or make a small purchase, all the better. At 10 a.m. first shift security unlocked the remaining mall doors and the retail day began in earnest.

On weekdays, mall customer flow was fairly predicable. Just as the walkers were departing, the stroller brigade arrived – young parents, grandparents and care providers with babies and preschoolers. For this group, visiting the mall wasn't about the shopping. The stroller brigade used it as a place to escape for a couple hours, sometimes in the company of other parents and tots. Their presence made for easy work for the morning security staff: lost teddy bears, a band-aid for a tiny finger, a friendly presence in the parking lot while diaper bags, strollers and kids were unloaded or loaded into vans.

As the stroller brigade hurried away at the lunchtime-naptime hour, they were replaced by the local office employees who arrived between noon and 2 p.m. for a quick lunch from the food court or to make a fast purchase before returning to work.

Then the morning security shift departed just as the after school teens began streaming into the mall bringing with them their parent's credit cards and their own special set of security problems. Second shift security guards – poor devils – got to handle the teenagers and every other security issue until the mall closed for the night. It was no secret that second security shift resented the first and third shift employees. All three shifts worked from the same pay scale but second shift definitely had the toughest workload.

Teens and their social behaviors permeated second shift. Fights, romances, noise, angst, frivolity, pent-up energy, and all their backpack-iPod-cell phone-drug stash-makeup-small weaponry paraphernalia accompanied teens into the mall. On any given day they could be a happy group or an angry gang, a delight or a horror show. The teenage presence continued at varying levels until closing time every day of the week. Second shift saw the most shoplifting, but teens were mostly involved in petty theft, not the organized heists. Unfortunately, all shoplifting cases, regardless of value, were time-consuming. Each required security staff to question, potentially search, and then detain suspects until local authorities arrived to make an arrest.

The number of mall visitors swelled during second shift. The post-work crowd began arriving soon after five o'clock. Hoards of tired and hungry children were dragged through the mall by tired and hungry parents.

As mall-weary family groups and tired single shoppers departed to collapse at home, the last wave of mall visitors wandered in. Every evening at closing time, people came to meet friends, lovers or family members who worked at the mall. Occasionally on weekends, an inebriated adult male accompanied by an inebriated female escort would stagger in for some last minute shopping. They were easy to pick out, and likely to make three stops: First, the automatic teller machine where the man would make a series of withdrawals, handing the money over his shoulder to the lady standing behind him. The recipient of the cash was invariably younger, taller, and thinner than the gentleman and her accessories included lots of hair, heel height, long nails, makeup, and jewelry. Their second stop was the lingerie shop for a purchase placed in the smallest of shopping bags. The final stop was at one of the mall's many jewelry stores where the woman would select – and the man would pay for – a necklace, bracelet, anklet or pair of earrings featuring at least one precious stone. Sometimes intervention by security was necessary when disagreements ensued, usually at the jewelry counter.

At closing time most mall patrons headed directly to the exits and their cars. Second shift guards herded any stragglers to the doors and checked all areas to assure that everyone – customers and merchants alike – had left the building before final lockup. Some nights it was an easy job. Other times, less so.

One tough task involved ushering out the homeless man known to security as Baby-Biker-Boy. Baby-Biker-Boy could spend an entire day on the same bench in the mall reading, humming, eating, and sleeping. He was unkempt and his behavior was unconventional but orderly. His sources for the extravagant, raggedy retro clothes he wore and the wide variety of books he read were a continuing mystery. One day he might be wearing a threadbare brown corduroy suit with a battered felt fedora and reading an antiquarian medical textbook. Another day he might be reading a children's book about Rome and dressed as though he'd just left the set of the old Sonny and Cher Show. His mall visits were always more frequent and longer whenever outside temperatures were below freezing. At the end of the day, security would move Baby-Biker-Boy to an exit and offer to call the local shelter to come pick him up. Although they always made this offer, he never wanted to go to the shelter. So the guard stood at the door and watched Baby-Biker-Boy heft his heavy backpack onto a shoulder – a beat-up old baby doll protruding from the top – and ride off into the darkness on his rickety bicycle, giving the peace sign to everyone he passed.

Another more challenging closing-time nuisance for mall security reoccurred every spring. Incidents of high school kids hiding in the mall after closing blossomed like daffodils. The security staff referred to the hiding teens as "Easter eggs" since the occurrences picked up around Easter time. Sometimes teens hid in the mall on a dare. Sometimes a teenage couple ("egg and chick") would decide it might be cool to spend the night. After years of these cases, security knew all the many hiding places kids used. The perennial challenge was some stealthy kid moving from place to place inside the mall, successfully avoiding the guards. When one of those was on the loose ("an Easter egg roll"), the situation got left for third shift security to handle. Few Easter eggs ever made it through the entire night. Security usually caught up with the hideaway in a bathroom, or at an exit when the kid decided in the middle of the night that he'd had enough and unknowingly triggered a silent door alarm.

The two-person overnight mall security crew arrived by 11 p.m., just as the second shift was packing up to leave. At that time of the night, the mall was empty and the lights were dimmed. There were rules about not sleeping on the job and getting caught could result in immediate dismissal. Drinking, gambling, or bringing guests into the mall were also against the rules. The temptations were greatest for overnight shift employees. After all, who was looking when the mall was closed? But the third shift sometimes forgot that the departing second shift workers were watching as shifts changed, and third shift workers had been observed bringing pillows into the security office. Disgruntled second shift employees would periodically snitch on the activities of the third shift security team when things got out of hand. Like the time a third shift guard arrived with a case of beer and a hooker. Or when the poker table, Jack Daniels and cigars were set up before second shift was even out the door.

The event that stirred Brad Mather's peptic ulcer that hot Monday morning in mid-August didn't come his way from a disgruntled second shift security team. No, this Monday's bad news began with a phone call from mall manager Ted Greene who described to Brad some strange scenes discovered by the morning security shift at his mall.

Vendors in the food court reported pilfering from their food storage facilities, scattered cups, soda spills and footprints through the mess; but no serious theft or damage. There were several large puddles of water on the floor around the central fountain. So far no leaks had been detected that would have caused the standing water. Also, the two quiet young security guards who had been hired last spring to work third shift were not on duty when the first shift staff arrived.

Ted told Brad that he was still taking reports and finishing a complete rundown on the facility, but there appeared to be no signs of a break-in or other foul play.

"I've been calling the home numbers of the two missing guards, but there's no answer," the mall manager told Brad. "I figure I'll send someone to their apartments before I report them missing. I'd sure feel foolish if it turns out they're at home asleep in their own beds."

"Good idea." Brad had the phone to his ear and his eyes closed tight as he listened. He was rubbing his face and hoping this all turned out to be nothing, but his stomach was telling him not to get his hopes up.

"Oh, and one more thing," the mall manager was saying. "I still need to take a look at last night's security tapes. I'll let you know if anything shows up."

Brad felt a sharp stab in his gut with the mention of the security tapes. "OK, keep me posted and call me before you take any action." As he hung up, Brad was certain that whatever this was, it was unlikely to turn out well.

An hour later, the mall manager telephoned Brad with bad news. The evidence uncovered on the security tapes was tabloid worthy. A few years into the future and the video would have been choice fodder for YouTube.

The images on the tapes clearly showed the third shift security guards cavorting through the mall like boys at play. The sound featured wild laughter, snickering, fits of giggles and unintelligible conversation. Their adventures began shortly before 2 a.m. The security tape from the food court revealed the two men rolling over the counter at Tammy's Tacos, eating handfuls of chips and washing them down with soda slurped directly from the soda machines. As they proceeded to raid the cold-rooms of three other food court stalls, their actions began to resemble a couple of frolicking puppies, deep into trouble while their owners were away.

After leaving the food court, the time-stamped security tape from the mall's central atrium documented the guards' abrupt stop at the edge of the indoor fountain. The looks on their faces reflected a sense of discovery as though they had forgotten the fountain was there. They glanced at each other and whooped loudly in unison. Without exchanging a word the two guards quickly proceeded to remove food stained uniforms, shoes, socks, shirts, and the remainder of their clothing. They leaped into the shallow water of the fountain and splashed about as though they were in a community kiddy pool. Naked, thin and pale, the guards looked even younger than the ages on the paperwork in their personnel files.

Suddenly one of the guards stopped splashing and looked down in the water at his feet. He waded back to the pile of clothes and extracted his white tube socks, then splashed over and gave one sock to his companion. Holding the sock in one hand, he started scooping something out of the water and putting it in the sock – the Make a Wish change from the floor of the fountain.

Over the next fifteen minutes of tape the naked guards worked furiously to fill their socks with the wet coins. When all four socks were full to bursting, the guards got dressed quickly and together let themselves out through the security exit. The tape from outside the exit door showed the young men talking and laughing as they walked away into the night with a bulging sock hanging from each fist. Their demeanor resembled teens completing a successful shopping trip. Nothing about their mannerisms, gestures or actions suggested any sense of self-consciousness, responsibility or stealth.

By the end of the business day Brad ordered the tapes overnighted to headquarters via Fed Ex. He instructed Ted to show the tapes to no one and to make no copies. He also suggested to Ted that his job security as the mall's manager would be best assured by keeping quiet about the events of the day.

The mall manager had guessed right. The missing guards were at home sleeping off whatever intoxicant they had drunk, smoked, sniffed or ingested. The socks full of change were easily recovered. Later that day the two young men were asked to sign papers resigning their jobs in exchange for keeping quiet about what they had done. Although there were discussions about pressing charges, it would have only resulted in bad publicity for the mall and The Easton Company.

Before going home for the evening, Brad took a walk down the hall to the office of Bill Briggs, the company's security director. He shut the door and shared with Bill the details of the security guards' overnight romp.

"It's hard to know whether to scream or laugh," Bill said to Brad. "I keep waiting for you to say April Fools or something. We screen, we train, we think we've made good hires and then we have something like this. I'll book the training room for tomorrow at noon and we'll watch the tapes together behind closed doors."

"Right," Brad laughed for the first time all day. "Will you bring the popcorn or shall I?"

In his role as corporate security director, Bill placed one last late day call to the mall manager to reinforce the "lips sealed" status on the entire fiasco. The instructions were clear: code of silence on this for anyone with any knowledge of the facts. Bill also instructed Ted to place follow-up calls to the fired guards at home that evening to emphasize the consequences of discussing with anyone (even family) what had happened the previous night. If they talked at all, they would find themselves quickly charged with a number of crimes and looking for bail money. Bill wanted those boys scared good and quiet – no bragging about their escapade over beers in the local bar.

What Bill didn't realize, but the mall manger had his suspicions about, was that the guards had virtually no recollection of their own adventure. Whatever substance they had employed to reach their childlike euphoric state had left them with little memory of what they had done. Wisely, the full details had not been shared with them – only that their shameful behavior had included stealing money from the fountain, abandoning their posts, and causing damage in the mall. Bill and Ted agreed that if luck prevailed, they just might successfully bury this one.

Say It Out Loud

Kate Cooper and her husband Matt were in the habit of taking long walks around the lake in the park adjoining their neighborhood. During those after dinner walks, they talked through the events of the day, discussed work, the children, friends, family, and current events.

One August evening on a walk that started at twilight, Kate said out loud to her husband something she had been thinking about for the past few days.

When Matt asked, "How was work?"

She answered, "I think they're going to sell the company." It had been on her mind since the end of last week and now she thought how strange it was to finally voice the idea.

"What?" Matt abruptly stopped walking and turned to look her in the face, as though she were some crazy woman instead of his wife of twenty-five years. "What are you talking about?"

"Keep walking," Kate instructed and took Matt's arm to encourage his forward motion. "It's just a feeling I have. Well, not just a feeling. It's based on some things I've been observing at work recently. It's not just what's going on – it's what's not going on."

"Like?"

"Suddenly the pieces are fitting together. First – out of the blue last week – a decision was made to delay plans for benefits open enrollment for a month. Larry Baxter has been sequestered in his office for weeks. He seems to be working on more projects than I've ever seen him tackle. It looks like lots of spreadsheets and data collection. Every now and then he asks one of us for some obscure fact or bit of information. The staff keeps asking him if there's anything we can help with, but he just looks at us angrily and says no. That's not like him. Normally, he'd be delegating that kind of project work to

T.J. or me or one of the other managers. Instead, he's in his office looking frantic, surrounded by stacks of papers and files."

"Yeah, well, but we both know the man's an odd duck, Kate," Matt responded.

"But a shrewd one. Not someone to get stuck with doing work he hates when he has a huge staff to delegate to. It's not normal."

"Haven't you seen this behavior before?"

"Yes, when we're getting ready to acquire another company. But on those projects Larry brought in his top four directors to help, swearing us to secrecy. It looks like the same type of activity, but he's holding it close."

"Maybe you're no longer in the loop. Maybe he's stopped trusting you for some reason."

"Could be. But if so, he's stopped trusting all of us. None of us have said anything to each other except to whisper the occasional 'What's going on?' when some question Larry is asking seems out of character."

"You're starting to sound like T.J., the corporate conspiracy theorist."

"Yeah, well. Given today's events, it may turn out that T.J.'s predictions weren't so crazy after all."

"What happened today?"

"You know the wellness fair we've been working on for two months? The one that's scheduled for the first week in September?"

"Yeah."

"Larry cancelled it. The space was booked, the staff had lined up dozens of vendors and community organizations and health care specialists for the booths. We had fitness demos scheduled and hired a seated massage therapist who was willing to give us her time at half her normal rate. Marcie even managed to snag a national wellness speaker for the luncheon. The guy normally charges $3,000 for an hour presentation, but because he's a good friend of Bing Sullivan, he offered to speak for free."

"Did Larry say why he was canceling it?"

"No. That's the weird part. He walked in my office today and asked me a question about our 401(k) plan funds. After I gave him the answer, he turned to go. Then he turned back and said, 'Oh yeah. By the way. You need to postpone the wellness fair.' When I asked why, he said it conflicted with some other events on the corporate calendar and we could look into possibly rescheduling it next year. When I asked what events he was referring to, he never gave me a specific answer. Just said Jeffrey Elkins told him to cancel it. Which is strange, since we had initially cleared the dates with both corporate activities and with Gloria, Jeffrey Elkins' secretary who keeps the master schedule. When I called Gloria this afternoon to ask what had been added to the corporate calendar on the eighth of September, she said she wasn't aware of anything other than the wellness fair."

"I see. That's odd and depressing. But Kate, stranger things have happened before."

"So you keep reminding me."

"Isn't this just more in the continuing saga of A Day in the Life of Corporate America?" Matt teased. "Remember the time Larry asked you to postpone your knee surgery because they were hiring a new chief operating officer? And how many times has he asked if you could cancel a vacation to accommodate the latest crisis?"

"I know. But I've always known why I was being asked to do something, whether I agreed with it or not. That's the reason I've been keeping my thoughts to myself these past few days. I guess what happened late this afternoon was the event that made me think this is something bigger."

"What happened?"

"You know how Larry only goes out of town on vacation for two weeks each year? The beach weeks in August?"

"Yeah. When you all celebrate not having him in your hair by playing loud music and throwing wild parties," Matt teased again.

"Oh very funny. Larry always books a beach house for his family during the same two weeks every summer, when Jeffrey takes his August vacation. He's supposed to leave this Friday. On his way out this afternoon, Larry stopped by my office and said, 'By the way, I won't be leaving for vacation on Friday.' When I asked why, he said he was hoping to join his family for the second week. Matt, the man never misses his two weeks at the beach. It's one of the few things he keeps sacred on his calendar."

"OK, but as I said before, he's asked you to cancel vacations."

"I know. But here's the rub. After that I got a call from Glen in finance about one of the nonqualified plans. Anyway, he mentioned that it didn't look like it was going to be the normal quiet August at Easton, since so many of the execs were canceling their vacations, including the CEO."

"Huh. So Elkins is staying in town and so are his executives," Matt reviewed.

"I figure it has to be something big, and it doesn't appear to be an acquisition. Yet it looks like acquisition activity. Except we've put so many projects on hold over the past few weeks, which has never happened before."

"So you really think they're selling?" Matt asked Kate in a voice that now almost sounded convinced.

"I know. It just seems too incredible to be true. And now that I've said it out loud, I sense I'm going to look foolish in the near future when this turns out to be nothing exceptional."

"It's an interesting speculation, I have to admit."

"Promise you won't repeat this to anyone, OK? I don't want this coming back to bite me," Kate said to her husband.

"I think this calls for another lap around the lake."

Security Matters – Tuesday

As Brad walked down the hall to the training room Tuesday morning with the Fed Ex package of security tapes under his arm, he felt like he was sneaking off to watch X-rated movies. Bill was waiting for him at the training room door.

The training room was a relatively new addition to the Easton headquarters building. It included all the latest sight and sound technology for high quality corporate presentations. The room had no windows and was sound insulated so well that when the electronically controlled doors slid closed some attendees experienced a brief moment of claustrophobia. The room was nearly square and relatively small, built to comfortably accommodate only a dozen people at one time. Labeled the training room, it was actually designed to provide an intimate setting free from outside distractions where Easton executives could sell investors on the wonders of the company's projects. Although no one would actually admit it, the walls, floor and ceiling were engineered to block cell phone calls and PDA reception.

Once inside the room, Bill pushed the button in the conference table console that closed the doors with an airtight whoosh. Then he loaded the first of the tapes into the VCR and hit play.

Forty-five minutes later the two men sat rubbing their faces as the last tape ended and the lights came up.

"I need coffee," Brad said.

"Screw that," Bill replied. "I need Scotch."

Between them they had more than thirty-four years of property management experience. Each had dealt with episodes of odd, absurd and sometimes frightening behavior by employees. Yet neither of them had ever witnessed anything quite like this. Seeing the actual footage of the two naked

90

security guards sp ashing around in a mall fountain was even worse than they had imagined. Brad had a creepy feeling that with the addition of a sound track he might have been watching the musical romp from one of those old Monkees TV shows.

"Do you think we've covered all the bases?" Brad asked. "Is there anything we haven't done that we should? Maybe we need to get on a plane and go out there."

"Maybe," Bill replied. "Although I'm not sure there's anything more we could do by being there other than quarantine everyone involved. Watching this has convinced me of one thing though. We'd best cover our asses and report this to Elkins. Better to take a little heat now and pray it all stays under wraps. Can you imagine if this were to leak out and get to the CEO through other sources?" Bill turned and picked up the receiver on the conference room phone. "I'll put us on speaker just as soon as I'm sure he's in."

"So much for this year's bonus," Brad mumbled.

"Trust me on this one. We control the story as long as we're doing the telling. That wasn't you and me romping around in that fountain."

Jeffrey Elkins was in his office when Bill's call came through. Except for his intense breathing into the phone, he listened quietly as Bill carefully summarized the situation.

Bill concluded with, "In any event, we believe we've taken the appropriate measures to contain the situation and avoid any press. However, we want to be certain there isn't any other action you want us to take at this time." Elkins was still quiet on the other end of the line, prompting Bill to offer, "Would you like to see the tapes sir?"

The gruff forcefulness of the CEO's answer made both men jump.

"Christ, no! Absolutely not."

"OK sir."

"I want those tapes destroyed now – within the hour. And not another person is to see or hear about any piece of this, do you understand me?"

"Yes sir," Bill crisply responded. So much for his brief fantasy about using an excerpt from the tapes in a future security management training film.

Security Matters – Friday

Three days after Brad Mather and Bill Briggs watched the security tapes in the training room, the sale of the company was announced. Late that morning, Bill walked down to Brad's office and leaned in his doorway.

"Hey, Brad. Can you believe it? And we thought the beginning of this week was a doozie."

Brad was in the process of extracting books from the shelf behind his desk and piling them into a large cardboard box. He turned and grinned at Bill.

"No wonder Elkins was seething through the phone. Can you imagine how a news story about Easton security guards dancing naked in a fountain might have affected the negotiations with Pratt-Miles?"

"Dancing naked, inebriated and on XTC while on the clock," Bill added.

"Good point."

"Elkins would have had us drawn, quartered and served for dinner," Bill concluded. Brad dropped another book into the box on his desk.

"You're not packing already are you?" Bill asked.

"Indeed I am. Packin' for the pink slip," Brad replied almost gleefully. "Pratt-Miles already has a corporate property manager, so my days here are numbered."

"That's not what I'm hearing," Bill answered with one eyebrow raised. "The way I hear it, you're not going anywhere."

Brad looked puzzled.

"Your rep precedes you, man. I got a call this morning. They may want you to go back into mall management. Word is out that you're the best around. Looks like you can kiss that severance check goodbye."

Brad's stomach churned. "Severance check or not I'm out of here," he said without missing a beat in placing another book in the box. "My work here is done."

Bill laughed out loud. "You've got to be kidding. They're sure to offer you a great salary and give you some prime location. San Diego, or maybe Vegas. You may even get to choose. Come on Brad. Get real. What the hell else would you rather be doing?"

Smiling again, Brad stopped packing and looked up at Bill. Then he glanced at the volume he was holding in his hand.

"Actually Bill, I think I'd rather write a book."

PART FOUR

IN THE WEEKS AFTER THE ANNOUNCEMENT

In the News

August 17

CORNERSTONE LOST

WASHINGTON (USAMedia) – County Executive Norris McMannis was still in high school when Ed Easton began developing what was then referred to as the "New American City," a grand experiment in community living that became a catalyst for the Washington area's suburban growth.

More than thirty years later, when told of the impending sale of The Easton Company to a Denver corporation, McMannis froze. Imagine Silicon Valley without Apple or Florida without Disney.

"I just sat there and looked at the message handed to me, saying; 'Is this real?'" said McMannis. "I was just shocked."

Within hours, shock among the region's political and civic leaders gave way to unease as they tried to fathom the likelihood of losing the Easton headquarters and some or all of the nearly 400 jobs housed there. This is an institution revered for decades as one of America's most innovative corporations.

By yesterday afternoon, financial analysts described the deal as good for shareholders, but not good for northern Virginia.

While Pratt-Miles will no doubt carefully sift through the Easton portfolio, closer to home many will be wondering about the fate of Easton's contemporary office building, set on a beautiful man-made lakefront and designed by the renowned architect David Sinclair.

Stewart Fitzgerald, a long-time resident of the area, said he, like almost everyone he knows in the community, was surprised by the news. And yet there was a sense of inevitability about the company's departure from the area, he said.

"I think we knew that one day this was going to happen. We just didn't think it would be so soon," Fitzgerald said.

Short Ride on the Gravy Train

On the Monday after announcement day in Easton's employment department, Terry Kagan walked into the office of his fellow recruiter Sean Maxwell and said, "OK. Now I get it. The veil has been lifted. The cataracts removed from my eyes, the clouds have cleared. I am enlightened."

"Now we finally know why the vice presidents were hiring their cronies for high paying, apparently non-existent jobs," Sean replied.

"Hate to say it, but I wonder what the VPs were getting in return."

"Hey, keep your voice down. You don't want Larry to hear us."

Terry laughed. "You're kidding, right? What's he going to do? Fire us? Oh, snap. I wouldn't want that to happen. We're about to be placed at the front of the layoff list my friend. One thing a new owner doesn't need or want is the other company's employment staff. We're about to be as un-busy as the three guys we were just discussing."

"Yeah, but the difference is no one's going to hand us a severance check anywhere near the size of the ones for those three invisible newbies."

Terry sighed. "What I wouldn't give for a ticket to ride on that lucrative gravy train."

Only the Dogs

What is it like to be a public figure with a shy and private personality? Jeffrey Elkins relished his privacy, but after the announcement of the sale of the company, he felt exposed. He knew the announcement would be a major business news story. But Jeffrey hadn't anticipated his name splashed about the city paper's editorial page and featured in the national news with that $90 million figure attached to it. With all the coverage, Jeffrey Elkins cringed to think that so many people whose names he did not know and did not want to know were thinking and talking about him.

The local news virtually deified the deceased Easton Company founder and the inevitable comparison made Jeffery's $90 million haul seem grubby. He felt vilified by the undertone of the local newspaper's editorials, casting him as a miserly Ebenezer Scrooge counting his coin. That certainly wasn't him. He saw himself as a Renaissance man, lover of art, theater, fashion and history, not the anti-hero in what was simply a business decision.

Once the announcement was made Jeffrey's phones rang nonstop; he eventually unplugged the home lines to get some peace from the stream of friends, colleagues and family who were calling to get the details about the deal directly from him. He was tired of talking about it. Forty-eight hours following the announcement, Jeffrey walked outside his house and dropped his cell phone into the trash bin.

While his wife escaped to her art council meetings, Jeffrey took refuge in their home gym lifting weights. He had never been the athletic type nor cared much for sports beyond the requisite corporate golf outing; although when his own boys were growing up playing lacrosse and soccer, Jeffrey enjoyed attending their games and celebrating their sports accomplishments. Then in the past few years, as he started experiencing more intense stress in his life, he began paying attention to his own health. This introspection resulted in a number of changes to his routine, including the addition of an extensive home workout facility and triweekly visits by a personal trainer.

Like so many others, Elkins had been forever changed by the events of 9/11. His youngest son, a trader on Wall Street, was at work in lower Manhattan that morning. It had taken several hours to reach him and confirm his safety. During those same hours Jeffrey was dealing with devastating news concerning one of Easton's landmark properties adjacent to the World Trade Center. Two employees died in the collapse and several others were seriously injured. The fear and stress he experienced that day triggered an entirely new set of worries to add to an already extensive list.

In the weeks after 9/11 Jeffrey was distracted, out of sync, and found it difficult to concentrate. Seemingly overnight, he had a new crop of gray hair. He cancelled his weekly hair trim, and disregarded his general appearance. Some days he forgot to shave. People began to worry and then to talk.

It was his wife, Anne, who eventually took charge and guided Jeffrey back into focus. In late October she hired a personal trainer for him. Then she sent him away for a long weekend at a very private, exclusive men's resort and spa for a regimen of massage, tanning, hair treatment, and more. He had come home from that experience feeling reenergized and renewed. Anne announced that if exercise and spa treatments didn't do the trick, she would schedule an appointment for him to see a female psychologist friend of hers – a fate Jeffrey would avoid even if it meant faking part of his recovery. By Thanksgiving, when the children came home, he was back to his old self emotionally, and in better shape physically than he had been in years.

In the days following the announcement that Easton was being sold, Jeffrey's life changed again. Associates, friends and family – even his wife – began treating him differently. In addition to his impending graduation to a new level of wealth, the demonstrated power to change the future of a Fortune 500 corporation was affecting how people thought about him. It was disturbing and he didn't like it.

Jeffrey Elkins had always been somewhat aloof, even with his closest friends. He was not one to share intimacies, personal stories, or life experiences. Now that the company's sale was news, he felt his personal life invaded as others were obviously reassessing him and passing judgment. It occurred to Jeffrey that Anderson & Sheppard, his Rhodesian Ridgebacks, were the only living creatures in his life unaware of his newfound power and wealth. At least the dogs still greeted him the same as ever.

In the News

August 19
Op Ed – Washington Chronicle
Big Payday

Last week brought us one more reminder about the power of the privileged few with the announcement of yet another colossal corporate merger. Americans have never particularly liked corporate giant-making. A century ago, Americans outraged by the excesses of industry robber barons actually wrote into law a wide range of antitrust rules designed to prevent corporate concentration. Over the past quarter-century, these rules have essentially become obsolete. The latest evidence: Friday's unveiling of a new multibillion-dollar mega-merger between Pratt-Miles and The Easton Company.

Mergers these days, in whatever sector they take place, invariably come with corporate news releases celebrating the "synergy" and "economies of scale" the new couplings create. By economies of scale, of course, the merger partners mean layoffs. Among the surest merger casualties: mid-level headquarters jobs. Who benefits from mergers? The biggest beneficiary from last week's dance between Easton and Pratt-Miles will be the Easton CEO who cut the deal. Easton CEO Jeffrey Elkins stands to pocket at least $90 million from the transaction. That would give Elkins what appears to be the biggest executive payday in Virginia history.

Change in Control

Change in control. In mergers and acquisitions, there is no phrase more powerful. Change in control refers to a change in ownership or control of a company triggered by one of the following events: someone grabs a significant block of the company's voting stock; the company's existing board members are no longer the majority on the board of directors; a merger is completed; or the shareholders approve the sale of the company.

Once the event occurs, change in control becomes a modifier for other nouns. Foremost is the change in control group – employees blessed with change in control executive agreements. The change in control group is often synonymous with the company's key executives, the most senior dynamic dozen or so individuals whose rank and value to the organization qualify them to parachute out when the company is turned over to new owners.

The change in control agreements are the official parachute documents. It's common for such agreements to run twenty or more pages and include not just a list detailing the parachute payments, but also the terms under which the payments will be made. There are pages of definitions, but frequently there is no definition of "Executive." The language used in executive agreements often reaches the pinnacle of legalese. Every sentence requires intense parsing to gain a vague sense of the true meaning, and the sensational details are not revealed until the attachments. This is why savvy' document reviewers flip to the end of a document and work backward.

In each Easton executive agreement, the body of the document listed all the types of benefits and compensation comprising the total executive parachute payment. However, the actual number – the total cash value of those payments – was not revealed until the final page. There was a hierarchy within the group and not everyone's parachute had the same value. Yet the lowest ranking members of the change in control group were scheduled to receive a cool $1.3 million.

To punctuate the point, the last sentence in the final attachment to each executive agreement included this statement: The Total Executive Payments calculated in accordance with Section 10 of the Agreement as of immediately following the merger transaction are $252 million.

In the News

Local news stories after The Easton Company's sale announcement offered a wide range of sarcasm, anger and criticism. A Baltimore reporter who had done his research authored an especially terse, yet noteworthy, article.

August 22
Harbor TIMES
The Golden Rule – He Who Has the Gold, Rules

Last Wednesday must have been a really busy day for top bosses at The Easton Company.

They signed new golden parachute deals that would pay them big money just in case Easton got sold to another company and they lost their jobs.

Then their board agreed to sell Easton to another company – Pratt-Miles.

Potential…and fruition. Wishes…and fulfillment. All by the close of business last Friday. Dump that magic carpet; corporate executive Aladdin now has a better ride that floats through the sky.

Golden parachutes have been described as job insurance for top executives. But the last minute execution of the Easton executive agreements is like buying a storm policy the moment the hurricane blows your roof off.

In this era of acquisitions when corporations often get gobbled up by rivals, the thinking goes that bosses need extra incentives not to reject a takeover offer beneficial to shareholders just to protect their own jobs. But these days top executives are stockholders, often holding mountains of shares and options. How much more incentive do they need?

Where golden parachutes once were theoretical, contingent propositions, more and more they look like opportunistic piling-on, struck when takeover deals are already in sight. Maybe they're even becoming routine merger paperwork.

Easton is the third mid-Atlantic company in recent months to grant nice parachutes just before agreeing to a merger transaction that would potentially trigger them.

One truly must give credit to the rank-and-file employees of a soon-to-be-acquired company. Theirs is a character-building experience. To read such an article as this over morning coffee and still have the motivation, loyalty or integrity to proceed to their hourly paid jobs requires generous amounts of civility, self-control, grace, and an appreciation for the good things in life that money can't buy.

The Pilot's Story

Exiting the Hawker together after a flight back from Denver in early August, pilot Jake Martin accompanied Jeffrey Elkins to his waiting limo to say goodbye. The driver was walking around to open the rear door for the CEO when Jeffrey turned back to Jake and said in a low but casual voice, "A confidence, Jake. We may be in the news soon. Some things are about to change – but not for us. You'll still be flying for me when the dust settles." Then shaking Jake's hand he finished, "I'll be in touch," slid into the back of the limo and was gone.

"Odd," Jake muttered to himself as he walked back toward the hangar. "Who's 'we' I wonder." It was definitely a puzzler. Jake, like Jeffrey, was a man of few words. Normally, he could easily decipher Elkins' shorthand speech patterns. But this comment seemed to have no context to pin it to. It was nothing to lose sleep over, Jake concluded as he walked back to his office to complete his post-flight paperwork before heading home.

Within a week came the announcement about the sale to Pratt-Miles. During the thirteen weeks between the announcement and the actual sale, Jake only flew Jeffrey once. He transported the CEO and his wife, Anne, to Florida for what Jeffrey referred to as some needed R&R. During those flights down and back, the couple read quietly and rested. There was no discussion with the pilot about the sale of the company. The Elkins only exchanged brief pleasantries with Jake as they entered and exited the plane.

Jake had sufficient military experience not to ask questions or worry. To Jake, the news of the sale was interesting, but a minor drama. He trusted Jeffrey and was enjoying the down time.

For Your Eyes Only

When the vice president of human resources asked Barbara Mallery, the corporate payroll manager, to step into his office and shut the door, Barbara had some idea what to expect. Eight weeks had passed since the Easton sale was announced and everyone in HR knew the merger talks with Pratt-Miles were progressing on schedule.

"Sit down," Larry Baxter said to Barbara. This was a rare event. Larry seldom wanted anyone to stay long enough in his office to take a seat. He was the terse, cut to the chase type. But Barbara was just the opposite. She was a master of detail and it drove Larry nuts. So being invited to sit meant something important was about to be discussed.

As prologue, Larry proceeded to give Barbara a mini-lecture reminding her about the ever-present need for confidentiality – a topic about which Barbara was fully cognizant. As payroll manager, she alone knew more about the cash flow of the employee population, especially the senior executives, than anyone else in the company. Barbara's responsibilities exposed her to executive tax records, child support garnishments, special pay arrangements, and much, much more. Where money matters intersected with messy lives, the facts ended up in payroll. An active member in the American Payroll Association, Barbara taught a night class in payroll ethics at the local community college. She really didn't need anyone lecturing her on the topic. But given the circumstances – the current pending sale of the company – she sat quietly nodding. If Larry felt the need to reinforce his status and rank versus hers, she'd let him. It didn't change the fact that Barbara was the subject matter expert on payment of executive compensation triggered by merger. She had already been through two other large corporate mergers in her payroll career and probably knew more about the compensation aspects of these deals than anyone in the human resources group; possibly more than anyone in the company.

"...So you see," Larry concluded, "what I'm about to give you is for your eyes only." Larry then handed Barbara an unsealed bright blue Tyvek envelope with Barbara's initials and "#13" neatly printed in dark blue ink on the front. Inside Barbara found the change in control executive payout list and related documents: all the parachutes, special payments, bonuses, stock incentives, supplemental plans, vacation payouts, and other benefits each member of the change in control group would receive on the day the deal finally closed. Barbara gave the first page a quick once-over.

"Will I also be getting this electronically?" she asked as she noticed the number thirteen boldly printed in blue Sharpie at the top right hand corner of the first page.

"No," Larry replied. "Only paper copies are being provided to those who must see the information. You are not to copy or duplicate these in any way. You'll be receiving an email from the General Counsel's office about when the checks should be ready and how and where you will deliver them."

"If I have any tax questions, can I discuss them with someone in the Tax Department?"

"Absolutely not. If you have any questions or problems, come back to me and I will get the answers you need. Do not talk to anyone else but me about the contents of this document, even if you know they also have a copy. Your set of documents must stay with you at all times until you are done processing the necessary checks and tax records. Then you must return it all, sealed in its envelope, either to me or to the General Counsel, but preferably me."

Barbara nodded her head to indicate she understood. Larry continued to stare at her in such a way that she took it as a cue to leave. But as she began to stand up, Larry handed her another sheet of paper.

"One more thing," he said.

"What's this?"

"It's an agreement you need to sign acknowledging everything I just informed you about, along with the penalty provision for violating the agreement. Read it, sign it and I'll witness it."

Barbara was stunned. This was definitely a first in her merger experiences, but she realized she didn't really have a choice. The restrictions on her access and use of the information in the report were clearly stated along with the penalty that would be imposed if she did not proceed as instructed: immediate termination without severance. It was insulting, but she signed the agreement and stood up to leave.

"We're not done."

"Oh." Barbara exhaled as she slowly sat back down and carefully folded her large hands in her lap.

"You need to initial the bottom of each page of the document with this blue pen."

As Barbara flipped through the pages of the report, she saw the number thirteen in blue Sharpie repeated on each page and asked, "Who else has a copy of this?"

"You don't need to know that. But Jeffrey's copy is number one. Yours is number thirteen."

As Barbara scrawled her initials on every page she couldn't imagine anyone lower in rank than her who would need a copy. Even though she was a lowly manager, it was her payroll duties that necessitated her access to this high-level information. No doubt that fact galled Larry and some of the other members of the senior management change in control group.

"Thanks Barbara. That should do it for now."

As she walked back to her office, Barbara's thoughts were focused. The meeting with Larry had left her angry and offended. She'd like to see them legally and accurately process all these payouts without her. Like hell they could! There wasn't another person in the company who even understood the excise taxes imposed by IRS Code Section 4999 on these types of payments, much less all the other rules and regs that came into play. They could disrespect her all they liked, but in the end she would hold the purse strings until assurances were given that every single payout was in order.

Selling Park Place, Buying Decimal Place

In her office with the door firmly closed, Barbara Mallery sat bent over her desk reviewing the report Larry had given her. After an initial review, she started again from the beginning, carefully reading each section of text and digesting every number. Then she found herself in freeze mode, staring at one page of the report with her right hand poised over her calculator. After rereading it three times, she was still looking at page twenty-one, titled "Summary of Disbursements to be Made to the CEO Immediately Upon Completion of the Sale." Initially she thought there must be some mistake. These numbers couldn't be right. She had started to pick up the phone to call Larry and report the error. But she didn't. Her better judgment kicked in as her expert mind began to explore the possibility that the numbers on page twenty-one might actually be correct.

Barbara certainly wasn't naïve about executive compensation. She had seen some unbelevably large payments dispersed to top executives over the course of her career. She clearly understood that golden parachutes were not used as incentives for executives to jump in and rescue a situation. They were used by executives to bail out – usually leaving behind a disaster for the remaining employees.

In her payroll class, Barbara taught her students the history of golden parachutes. Originally, they were created to keep top executives from discouraging offers to buy the company, for fear of losing their own lucrative positions. By the twenty-first century, however, the intended design had backfired. Super-sized whenever a contract was on the table, parachutes had become part of the negotiation landscape leading up to an announcement of sale.

But these numbers. Good God. Her heart beat faster and she felt slightly ill. After staring at page twenty-one until she regained her focus, she let her

111

brain overrule her gut response and knew the figures must be correct. Barbara ran the CEO's numbers one more time just to be sure. With the CEO's list of payments now clearly imprinted in her mind, she knew what she had to do.

Barbara walked back down the hall to Larry Baxter's office and knocked on the door-jam. The blue Tyvek envelope was firmly gripped in her hand.

"Excuse me, Larry? Sorry to interrupt. But I need to speak with you again."

"Certainly," Larry replied, looking up from his laptop screen and wearing his steeliest poker face. "Come in."

He had been imagining Barbara's reaction as she read the report. Under the circumstances, Larry wasn't surprised to see her back so soon. Still, he was irked by her quick return. Her seemingly unending inquiries about every single task always made Larry's blood pressure rise. He loathed her probing questions about applicable federal and state income tax laws, IRS regulations, filing and withholding requirements, and all the related documentation. How he hated all that crap. It was particularly bothersome because he really knew very little about the subject, and only cared to know the details when it pertained to his own personal compensation situation.

Larry was familiar with the look now on Barbara's face. It was a look she consistently wore when she was about to deliver bad news. No wonder he hated it when this woman showed up at his office door. Discussions initiated by Barbara often ended with Larry making bad news phone calls to fellow executives, informing them about unanticipated withholding or some additional tax payments. These calls made Larry's peers foul-mouthed and ill tempered – and made him the focus of their anger. The head of human resources was such a shit job. These days, it caused any HR executive to be the primary punching bag for all the senior executives who despised the unending government regulations and red tape imposed on businesses.

"We have a problem," Barbara said softly and slowly without looking up.

Hearing those words, Larry cut her off. He was in no mood for her rambling minutiae.

"No Barbara," Larry exploded while quickly moving from his chair to shut his office door. "Not this time. Everything in the report has already been vetted, reviewed, and approved by three teams of lawyers, the accountants on each side of the merger, the finance and tax directors of both companies, and an SEC guidance expert. So, let's get this straight. There aren't any problems. We don't have any problems, despite questions you might have."

"Oh-kay," Barbara drew out the two syllables of the word, initially sending a sidelong glance in Larry's direction and then looked him straight in the eye without flinching.

There was a moment of silence in the office as Larry and Barbara glared at one another. When Larry realized Barbara might succeed in staring him down, he relented, "Alright Barbara. So what the hell's the problem with the numbers?"

Barbara broke her stare to flip to page twenty-one of the report.

"Oh, no problem with the numbers," she said in a newfound airy tone. "But we're going to need a new check printer."

"New check printer," Larry trilled. "What the hell for? We spent a small fortune on a new one just last year. I recall you told me it was top of the line for print speed, engine life, resolution, memory, capacity and connectivity. And we even got a multiyear warranty and service contract on the thing. It ended up costing us as much as the annual salary for one of your payroll clerks. So if it's broken, call and get it repaired or replaced. There is no way we're buying a new check printer now to run four or five more payrolls before the consolidation."

Struggling to suppress a grin, Barbara replied in the airy voice, "Oh, we'll definitely be needing a new one. But not to run payroll."

"What the hell is wrong with the one we have, for Christ's sake?" The volume of Larry's voice increased as the conversation continued. He was confused about what Barbara was getting at – but based on the cat-that-swallowed-the-canary look developing on her face, he was beginning to feel played.

Slyly glancing up from the report, Barbara answered Larry while looking him square in the face. She didn't want to miss seeing his reaction to the news she was about to deliver.

"We're going to need another decimal place. What's wrong with the printer we have? It prints a maximum of seven places to the left of the decimal. To print the CEO's parachute check, apparently we're going to need eight."

As it turned out, Larry Baxter was wrong to worry about discussing with Jeffrey Elkins the need for a new laser check printer. In the end, the CEO had no problem approving the $18,000 purchase order for the new printer with rush delivery and set-up. It would be used to accommodate the printing of just one check – his.

The Last Meet Up

Once the merger process was underway, Easton headquarters employees began seeing new faces in the building. Each week brought more Pratt-Miles staff flown in from Denver for fact-finding meetings with Easton executives. It wasn't long before an email went out from Lee Martino's office addressed to "Key Employees of The Easton Company." Many of the recipients were surprised to see themselves included on the list of invitees. Some granted themselves momentary permission to hope that they might enjoy some unanticipated special status in this merger. Others skeptically knew better.

The email announced a meeting to review merger planning and procedures. The list of email "key employees" caused recipients to wonder what type of information might be shared with a group ranking from CEO down to payroll manager. Oddly, except for Jeffery Elkins and Lee Martino, the change in control group was conspicuously absent from the invitation list. The twenty-three key employees asked to attend were both puzzled and curious. The impending sale of the company had plunged many of these individuals into a stunned state best described as floundering glumness. The email was a wake up call.

The email was sent less than forty-eight hours before the scheduled meeting, but nearly everyone attended and many appeared dressed for a job interview. Name placards had been placed on the large conference table and on the twelve additional chairs lined up in the rear of the room. The assigned seating resulted in some abnormal navigation as people attempted to locate their seats. Once seated, it was clear there was a hierarchy to the assignments, with the CEO and COO next to one another at the head of the table, department heads around the table, and function directors and the payroll manager in the chairs at the back. At each place was a seventeen-page handout that looked as though it had been quickly assembled – definitely not anything corporate communications had a hand in – thin white copy paper duplicated on a copier desperately in need of a toner cartridge replacement, and hand stapled in the upper left hand corner. The handout was titled: The Easton Company Merger Instructions for Key Employees – Highly Confidential. DO NOT COPY OR CIRCULATE.

Two function heads seated in the back tried not to snicker as one whispered to the other, "How would they know?" as she pointed to the faded DO NOT COPY text.

Once everyone was settled, the only person missing was Jeffrey Elkins. His name tent clearly labeled where he was supposed to be. Lee Martino checked his watch a few times, but at five after the hour he started the meeting without comment on the empty chair to his right.

"Thank you all for coming," Lee began. "As you know, the merger process has begun with Pratt-Miles assessing and evaluating not only our company assets, but also the processes, functions, and methodologies we use to run our business."

At that point the door opened and Jeffrey Elkins strode into the conference room. Lee paused and all eyes followed the CEO as he quickly moved around the table and took his place. Lee glanced sideways at Jeffrey whose eyes were fixed squarely on his name tent.

"Welcome," Lee said with a hint of sarcasm in his voice. Jeffrey gave a nearly imperceptible nod without shifting his glance from the tabletop.

"As I was saying," Lee continued, "The document in front of you is designed to provide some guidance over the next several weeks as Pratt-Miles goes through the process of pre-purchase discovery. Each of you has been asked to attend this meeting because you will play an important role in this discovery process." A few people shifted noticeably in their chairs, sitting up a bit straighter, listening a little closer.

"As department or function heads, you will likely be asked to meet with your Pratt-Miles peers and other representatives to answer questions about what you do and how you do it. First, let me say that we expect your full cooperation during this process. But let me be very clear. Cooperation does not equate to total access. There are certain lines here that should not be crossed without first consulting our legal team. It's not that we are attempting to hide anything during this process. Our books are open to Pratt-Miles during this period. However, what we all must keep in mind is that Pratt-Miles at this point is still our competitor. There is always a possibility that this deal could fall through."

Jeffrey now held his name card in his hands, rotating it slowly and carefully using both index fingers and thumbs. Those who could see his face thought they noticed the smallest smirk pass his lips. At that moment the tension between the two men seated at the head of the table was palpable. It was clear that the assigned seating arrangements had been some overeager

115

administrative assistant's nifty idea run amuck. Seating the CEO and COO shoulder-to-shoulder during this meeting had been a bad decision. Lee paused and the attendees shifted again in their seats, flipping pages in the handout.

"Bottom line here is you're all smart people. Answer the basics, but don't turn over any document without sending it through legal. Pratt-Miles is aware this is how things will be handled. All documentation requested will be catalogued, copied and sent to Denver once it has been screened by our attorneys."

This was the point in the meeting when it dawned on most attendees why they were there. It wasn't because they were special, important or key to the merger in any way that was noteworthy. All of them were mid and upper level managers – non-executives every one. They were present because the company needed them to be the workhorses a little while longer without screwing up the proceedings. Lee was working hard to make the people in the room feel like there would be an important role for them in the merger – that it was more than just an acquisition. The objective of the meeting, however, was to win cooperation from a set of employees with little to gain from "keeping up the good work" but whose help would be necessary during the transition. They were a group of employees who held needed information and performed very necessary administrative duties, but had no significant financial incentive to perform well during the run up to the sale.

"So please read through the handout and follow the instructions given. If you have questions let us know." Plainly, Lee had no plans to entertain questions during this meeting.

That didn't stop Barbara Mallery, the payroll manager, from raising her hand from the back row. "Mr. Martino?"

"Yes, Barbara," Lee sighed.

"What about payroll data? I've scanned the handout and there's nothing here that provides the kind of direction I need to determine what I should and should not provide during the discovery process."

"Good question," Lee rushed on, "but one I need you to take up with the legal team. Give Charles McKenzie a call when you get back to your office. I'm sure he can provide you the detailed guidance you need."

Any hope of an elevated status for the invitees in the room had been overblown. Given the content of the meeting, their appropriate places were evident.

Lee turned to Jeffrey and asked politely, "Anything you'd like to add, Jeffrey?" The CEO glanced toward Lee and when they made eye contact Jeffrey responded casually, "No. I think that covers it."

"All right then," Lee stood up, "thank you all for coming." The meeting ended and the group silently filed from the room.

It was the last time anyone present saw Jeffrey Elkins and Lee Martino speak to each other.

A Slice of the Pie

In the weeks between when a company announces its intention to merge and the date the merger actually closes, there is an interesting window of opportunity for investors. As usually happens when merger announcements are made, the stock price of the acquiring company goes down, while the price of the company being acquired goes up. The rationale here is easy to understand. The market knows that, in the short-term, the acquiring company will be spending time, energy and dollars to effect the merger; and it will be a year or more before the benefits of the merger will start showing up in their stock price. Meanwhile, on the other side of the merger, the company being bought has been offered more money per share than it is currently trading for – sometimes lots more per share. This is the so-called "spread." Assuming the merger goes through, stockholders have a short-term, near guarantee that the stock price will go up to the offer price by the date the deal closes. If the stock price falls due to financing concerns, or if the merger doesn't go through as planned, the stockholder may be disappointed. Still, many view the opportunity as a risk worth taking.

When a merger is in progress, an interesting subset of investors to watch are the 401(k) plan participants in the company being acquired. This is only relevant if the plan offers company stock as an investment choice. When merger announcements are made in these organizations, you can walk the halls of the company's offices and hear those calculators clicking. Everyone with options, shares or 401(k) dollars invested in company stock is doing the math. The halls of The Easton Company were no different. The same question was on the lips of dozens of plan participants calling human resources: "Is there a freeze on company stock fund trading in the 401(k) plan? If not, can I continue to buy and sell shares of Easton stock in my 401(k) account up to the day the sale closes?" Surprisingly, there were no restrictions. It was one of the few ways the little guys could get a piece of the last minute action.

With that answer in hand, plan participants were amazed that their Easton stock trading in the company 401(k) plan did not violate some insider-trading rule. After all, most management employees at corporate headquarters assumed they would have some clue if the merger unexpectedly headed south. A certain amount of caveat emptor still applied. If the deal fell through, the value of the shares would probably plummet. Still, if that happened, they might have time to sell before incurring losses.

Surprisingly, most Easton 401(k) participants did nothing with their plan investments in company stock. A handful chose to sell all their Easton shares as the close date drew near and the trading price increased toward the offer price. A small number bought a few more company shares in their 401(k) accounts as they witnessed the stock price begin to climb. Others chose to max out their annual 401(k) contribution amount with all the new money directed into Easton shares.

Only 3 participants out of nearly 2,000 bet the farm and moved all their 401(k) money into the company stock fund when the merger was announced. All three of these risk-takers were middle-aged males earning six-figure salaries, and they all worked in the Las Vegas sales office. This fact made human resources director Kate Cooper chuckle when she reviewed the weekly Trade Report for The Easton Company 401(k) plan. Unlike most Las Vegas players, these plan participants all hit the jackpot with their 401(k) gambles. Each had plan account balances in excess of $150,000 when the merger was announced.

One participant moved *all* his plan assets into the company stock fund, buying in at $34 a share. The stock paid out at $65 per share at close, just thirteen weeks later. His action netted him an increase of more than $136,000, nearly doubling his total tax deferred 401(k) account balance to just under $300,000 in those three months. The participant was amazed that the transaction was legitimate in the eyes of the Internal Revenue Service, the Securities and Exchange Commission, and Sarbanes-Oxley rules. This was certainly a serendipitous retirement planning vehicle no one had advised him about.

In the News

September 30
Developers Quarterly
Platinum Price Tag

Last month Pratt-Miles Inc. outmaneuvered two rivals to secure The Easton Company's gold star portfolio. And though Wall Street critics are suggesting that Pratt-Miles is paying platinum prices for its acquisition, Pratt-Miles CEO George Miles says the $13.1 billion price tag is well worth it.

Most of the facts concerning the auction process that resulted in Pratt-Miles' win are confidential, but a recent proxy statement Easton filed with the SEC reveals a few interesting details. For example, Easton executives approached Pratt-Miles and two other leading development companies to solicit bids after Easton CEO Jeffrey Elkins discussed possible sale of the company with George Miles over dinner in May. Following the conversation between Elkins and Miles, Elkins enlisted guidance from an international banking institution and a prominent brokerage firm to advise the company on a possible sale.

In July Easton contacted Pratt-Miles and another company ("Company A") to solicit bids in the $70-to-$75-per-share range. By mid-August Company A withdrew from the auction, citing a reluctance to rush the arrangement of financing. Two days later Company B – who had initially responded but then grew quiet through the bulk of the negotiations – re-entered the discussion, requesting that Easton delay the sale process so it could make an intervening bid in the $65-to-$70-per-share range. But Pratt-Miles put forth its formal offer of $65 per share that same day, and Easton's board voted to approve it rather than extend the bidding process. "Although both Company A and Company B had requested additional time to evaluate Easton and to present its best proposal, our board determined there were significant risks in extending the sale process," the proxy statement reads. Those risks included the possibility that Pratt-Miles might withdraw or reduce its proposal or that the bidders might decide to bid jointly.

One thing is clear: the deal is a watershed event in the development industry because of its size and because it is a cash transaction. If anyone had suggested ten years ago that a competitor would buy The Easton Company for $13.1 billion, they would have been laughed out of the room.

Pep Squad

Working for a company about to be acquired is an odd and unsettling experience. The stress can make even the most dignified employees do some very peculiar things. On an afternoon in early September, several long-service legal secretaries appeared on the lawn under the CEO's balcony and began conducting cheers The group of seven was dressed in white slacks, tunics and tennis shoes and carried green pom-poms. All were AARP eligible. Bouncing up and down they chanted:

"Gimme an E!"
"E!"
"Gimme an A!"
"A!"
"Gimme an S!"
"S!"
"Gimme a T!"
"T!"
"Gimme an O!"
"O!"
"Gimme an N!"
"N!"
"What's that spell?"
"EASTON!"
"What's that spell?"
"EASTON!"

Employees in the building migrated to the windows to see what the noise was about.

"What do we want?"
"Our jobs!"
"What do we need?"
"Our pensions!"
"When do we want 'em?"
"NOW!"

Some onlookers laughed and cheered along. Just as many found the display embarrassing and turned away.

"It's like watching my well-mannered mother make a fool of herself," one young man muttered.

The group repeated their repertoire of chants twice more, then clustered together and sang loudly in two-part harmony:

"We love you Easton
Oh yes we do
We love you Easton
And we'll be true
When it's all over
We'll be blue
Oh Easton how we've loved you!"

The watching employees hollered, clapped and whistled while the women took a bow.

Ten minutes later each cheerleader was back at her desk as though nothing out of the ordinary had occurred.

Once Upon a Time There Was a Merger and Other Fairy Tales

In late September, six weeks after the merger announcement, Easton stockholders received some interesting reading material in their mailboxes. Each was sent a proxy statement cordially inviting them to attend a special meeting of the stockholders held, not at the company's corporate headquarters in Virginia as was the usual practice for such meetings, but at the offices of a prestigious law firm in Manhattan. The meeting was scheduled for 9:30 a.m. on a Wednesday morning in early November. There would be no customary luncheon of Chesapeake Bay crab cakes, prime rib and strawberry shortcake that had always followed the annual stockholders meetings. This meeting had one purpose: to vote on a proposal to approve the merger of The Easton Company and Pratt-Miles. It was no surprise that the notice endorsed the merger and the Easton board of directors recommended stockholders vote FOR its approval.

The proxy statement was actually an eighty-page booklet containing a lengthy narrative of the merger bid process and the merger agreement, laced with statistics on who would get what in the deal. Tables reflecting the different executive compensation categories were liberally sprinkled throughout prudently labeled as "interests of certain parties" and "considerations to be received." The legally required language about rights, responsibilities and regulatory matters was layered at the end of the document.

Most stockholders never read beyond the section titled, "Consideration to be Received by Our Stockholders in the Merger" which confirmed in writing how much they would receive for their Easton stock shares. Some stockholders wanted to put their windfall in perspective, so they skimmed sections related to the executives' golden parachutes – although they certainly weren't labeled as such in the proxy. Still other stockholders who were former employees or Friends of The Easton Company read the entire booklet from cover to cover; some even read it a second time with a highlighter in hand.

It was in this proxy document that the reading public first learned The Easton Company had actually been auctioned off to the highest cash bidder. The entire process of securing a buyer for the $13 billion corporation had taken less than eight weeks, from initiation to sale announcement.

But Easton's retirees reading the proxy made a beeline to the one-page section labeled "Employee Benefit Matters." The transfer to Pratt-Miles of The Easton Company's benefit plans for non-executives was summarized in less than 500 words. A scant half dozen paragraphs conspicuously lacking specifics left much to the imagination – nothing at all like the level of detail contained in the sections addressing the executives' benefits. Some retirees found comfort in the opening sentence where Pratt-Miles agreed to honor The Easton Company's existing plans for a period of time after the merger. Reading a bit further, that comfort was banished by language that bluntly stated, "the continuation of existing benefits are subject to any amendment or termination permitted by law." So much for honor. Savvy retirees who were careful readers noted this section referred to "employee benefits" – there was no mention at all of retiree benefits. A handful of retirees felt relieved when they read that the new owner would "...provide benefits substantially similar, in aggregate, to benefits provided to similarly situated employees of Pratt-Miles." Most retirees did not learn that Pratt-Miles had no retiree benefit plans until months after they had cast their votes for the merger.

During the weeks between when the proxy statements were mailed and the scheduled meeting, local stockholders and employees mused about renting a bus and going to the meeting in Manhattan en masse. In the end, only a handful of stockholders made the trek to New York. It was just too expensive and too inconvenient.

For all their trouble, the stockholders who attended got to sit in a plush conference room in a high-rise on Madison Avenue where the coffee was served in white china cups. The meeting started promptly at 9:30 a.m. Eleven minutes later it ended before the coffee in the cups had time to get cold. Based on the results of the proxies received by mail, the vote on the final sale of the company had gone quickly, smoothly, and without discussion. More than two-thirds of the outstanding shares of Easton common stock had voted for the merger. Once those numbers were announced, there was no point in raising objections. The few stockholders who had actually planned to speak were easily intimidated from doing so. The meeting was adjourned. The stockholders present were thanked for their attendance and escorted to the exit.

"Well I never would have guessed," Linda said to her husband Greg as they rode down in the elevator with Ellen and Russ, who had driven to New

York with them for the meeting. The two couples were stockholders and Easton retirees.

As the foursome found themselves spit back through the skyscraper's revolving door onto bustling Madison Avenue, Greg asked, "So now what?"

"Christmas shopping," Ellen replied.

"Then lunch," Russ added.

"Somewhere nice?" Linda asked.

"Sure. Why not?" said Greg. "By the time the Visa bill shows up, it looks like we'll have some extra cash to pay for it."

In the News

FOR IMMEDIATE RELEASE
November 4
SHAREHOLDERS OF THE EASTON COMPANY APPROVE MERGER WITH PRATT-MILES INC.

N. Virginia – Officials of The Easton Company (NYSE:TEC) announced today that, at a special meeting of Easton Shareholders held this morning, the holders of more than the requisite two-thirds of its common shares approved the merger of a subsidiary of Pratt-Miles Inc. (NYSE:PMI) with and into Easton.

As Kate Cooper read the press release, it occurred to her that anyone reading this who had not been present for the special stockholders meeting probably assumed key information must have been purposely omitted or accidentally left out. But nothing more had happened during the eleven minute meeting.

The wording in the last line of the press release struck some as curious. That language about "…merger of a subsidiary…with and into Easton" gave new hope to some employees about who the actual power player might be in this deal. Some speculated that a significant portion of The Easton Company might independently survive when the merger dust settled. Others hoped the layoff rumors would turn out to be wrong and most of Easton headquarters employees would remain for the foreseeable future. Those who knew better than to be optimistic recognized the wording for what it was – legal mechanics required to pass the acquired "pig" through the tax and corporate "python" most efficiently. Once consumed, it would hardly be recognizable.

Spinning Plates

If anyone had bothered to ask Jeffrey Elkins to honestly describe how he was feeling during his last year as CEO of The Easton Company, he likely would have replied: "Stressed." Jeffrey had a mental picture of that stress. It was a picture he shared with no one, not even his wife. Near the close of his tenure as CEO, the visual was so vivid it became part of his dreams. At the end of his career, Jeffrey Elkins became a plate spinner – just like the performer on the old Ed Sullivan variety show who spun a dozen platters balanced atop tall poles. In recent years, Jeffrey was balancing more and more plates. The plates had names like corporate debt, 9/11, Sarbanes-Oxley, stockholder expectations, and skyrocketing employee medical costs. His dream became a nightmare where the plates were spinning so fast he couldn't even see the names on them anymore.

With all those spinning plates, Jeffrey was forced to constantly look up. There was no time or opportunity to do anything else but keep watching to make sure none of the plates stopped spinning.

Once he decided to sell the company, Jeffrey started having a new dream. In this dream he stopped looking up. He stopped spinning all those plates and just let them fall. In the new dream when the plates crashed to the floor Jeffrey felt such relief, he became gleeful – a state of being he had never before experienced in his entire life.

In the dream, when the plates crashed to the floor, it was clear that he was done spinning plates forever, and he could now leisurely look at the world around him. He could walk off stage and finally get the crick out of his neck from all those years of looking up.

Dreams of spinning and crashing plates summed up Jeffrey's perspective on the end of his career at The Easton Company. But Jeffrey Elkins was the only person who had this perspective. Long-service Easton employees, who had been with the company since the early days with Ed Easton as their CEO, held a dramatically different perspective. In just twenty-one weeks, Jeffrey Elkins had thrown away what they had spent thirty-five years building: a good and respected company with a solid reputation, a positive profile and a profitable balance sheet that kept thousands of people comfortably employed – including Jeffrey Elkins.

Moving Day

It came as no surprise to many in the company when – one week before the scheduled closing date to sell The Easton Company to Pratt-Miles – Jeffrey Elkins hired a private moving company to remove his antique office furnishings, one-of-a-kind artwork, and museum-quality personal possessions from the Easton headquarters building in the middle of the night.

Holiday Tradition

On the Tuesday before Thanksgiving for as long as Easton employees could remember, the company distributed a pumpkin pie to every employee at corporate headquarters. Not just any pumpkin pie, mind you. These beauties were trucked in each year from a boutique farmhouse bakery in Virginia's rural Piedmont hunt country. The pies were made from a hundred-year-old secret family recipe and the product lived up to the hype.

Each year the pies, boxed and tied with orange and brown organza ribbon, were delivered to employees' offices and cubicles by members of the corporate events staff along with a "Happy Thanksgiving" note from the CEO.

The order for the pies had been placed and paid for long before the merger announcement was made in August. However, it wasn't until a week before the scheduled merger close date that the director of corporate events realized she had a problem. That was when 400 preprinted Thanksgiving cards displaying an embossed Easton logo and Jeffrey Elkins' printed signature were delivered to her office. Once the stockholders voted for the merger, no one on staff thought to ask what should be done about the pies.

For Julia West, Easton's corporate events director, it was a "damned if you do, damned if you don't" situation. No one else had mentioned the pies, so obviously she wasn't the only one who had forgotten about them. She had three choices. She could say nothing and just distribute the pies as usual Thanksgiving week – maybe without the cards – and hope that her first phone call from the new management would not be about pies. Or she could ask for direction. But what senior executive did she dare bother with questions about pastry at this point in the merger? It crossed her mind that the best move might be to donate the pies to charity; but if the employees were to find out, it would be one more reason for them to feel morose and angry.

Julia put off taking any action for a few days, hoping someone would tell her she was on the list to be pink-slipped the day of the close. If that happened, she could walk away and the pies would be someone else's problem. Finally, she gave up hoping for divine intervention and emailed Gloria, Jeffrey Elkins' executive secretary, asking for guidance. Although no one had seen Jeffrey in the building for days, Julia was hopeful for some kind of response. Gloria copied Julia when she forwarded the email to Jeffrey but with only two days left before the close date, she knew it was futile.

Julia read the forwarded email and groaned. Pies, she thought. I'm bothering this man about pies when he's working on closing a $13 billion dollar deal. With my luck I'll be an early layoff victim, my name will forever be associated with the Thanksgiving pie fiasco, and Jeffrey Elkins will see to it that I never work in this town again.

What Do You Give as a Farewell Gift to a Guy Worth Ninety Million Dollars?

The Easton Company had a reputation for giving high quality gifts. Service awards, company anniversary commemoratives, holiday presents, stockholder meeting give-aways and even token mementos bore the names of Tiffany, Baccarat, Liberty, Channel and Gucci. With the sale of the company on track, it made sense for the executive board to begin discussing an appropriate parting gift for Jeffrey Elkins. Some board members were quietly shocked by the idea, while others seemed to think it appropriate to give him something in recognition of his effort to successfully sell the company. As one division head commented, "After all, he is making us multimillionaires."

The executive board was comprised of the company's senior vice presidents and corporate division heads. As they talked together and traded emails with ideas, the real issue revolved around how much each board member would contribute for the gift. Some thought each person should give equally, while the "lower paid" of the group suggested contributions based on a percent of each member's total compensation.

After several false starts and failed proposals, the group of ten senior executives decided to gift $100,000 to an inner-city private charter school that Elkins and his wife supported. The funds would establish a college scholarship in Jeffrey Elkins' name. Some executive board members quietly grumbled as they wrote their personal checks – but in the end, they were pleased with their gift to the CEO.

When the executives made their presentation at the last executive board dinner, Jeffrey was touched by the group's thoughtfulness and liked the idea of his name attached to something that would make his wife and family proud.

In return, Jeffrey gave each of the executives an antique lapel pin. Every pin was one-of-a-kind, stunningly jewel encrusted and uniquely designed. His wife's jeweler had selected each pin based on the personal profiles of the recipients. There were speeches, laughter and tears as the dinner progressed through the best regional food and French wine money could buy. When the evening ended, everyone felt special, privileged, and well feted.

The next day all the members of the executive board proudly wore their new pins. When one accountant complimented chief financial officer Lindsey Gordon on her beautiful ruby and diamond saber brooch, she smiled and replied that it was a gift from Jeffrey Elkins, mentioning that each division head had received one.

The Easton Foundation

Whenever a company is acquired, the local community suffers. Changes brought about by acquisitions generally result in declines in regional employment and operations. Small businesses suffer. Caterers, business supply stores, coffee shops, temp agencies, dry cleaners, car washes, lunch counters, office cleaners, landscapers – the list goes on – lose a major client or a significant number of regular customers.

Equally affected are community nonprofits. New corporate ownership brings new leadership, which affects area charities and other beneficiaries of the corporate citizenry. When a merger is actually a buyout or an acquisition and the acquiring company is from out of town, the local community loses.

CEOs become part of the fabric of their business and cultural community. Hometown companies that are thriving, along with their most senior management, often heavily support pet projects such as inner-city charter schools, performing arts venues, and a long list of annual events, charities and fill-in-the-blank-a-thons. In some organizations, corporate culture dictates that senior executives give away four or five percent of their compensation to charity. When the organization is a developer, those donations usually go to area philanthropic groups.

The Easton Company fit this mold. It sponsored and supported a variety of nonprofits ranging from community hospital fundraisers to 10K races and the symphony orchestra. A full-time Easton employee actively managed the company's charitable giving.

This type of corporate giving is accepted as normal business practice in the United States. When financial analysts crunch the profitability numbers to determine if the shareholder is being well served, corporate dollars to charities get a pass. They escape Wall Street scrutiny with the rationale that the money is going for good works. But how does this practice align with a corporation's mandate to put the financial interests of their shareholders above all else? Coincidentally, during the four years leading up to the Easton/Pratt-Miles merger, American corporations appreciably increased corporate giving budgets while simultaneously establishing that they could no longer afford to finance retiree pension and health care obligations for their employees, citing erosion of profitability. This statistic reflects an interesting shift in U.S. corporate priorities.

For the CEO about to sell a corporation, what better strategy than to inject into the deal not just a multimillion-dollar severance package for himself, but also a post-merger job as chairman of a newly established local foundation, funded with someone else's money. It's the ideal avocation for a former chief executive – managing and giving away five percent of the foundation's assets each year to favorite causes.

To appreciate the genius of this strategy, it's helpful to understand how nonprofit foundations are established and operated. Many large foundations provide significant donations to an array of good causes and worthy institutions. Foundations are funded with private money, but the source of the funding often has a clear and direct link to a for-profit corporation. It is unlikely there will ever be a help wanted ad to fill a foundation chairmanship, even in the most elite publications, and salaries for chairmen and presidents of foundations are usually not disclosed.

The multimillion-dollar contribution by Pratt-Miles to permanently establish The Easton Company Foundation was one part of the merger agreement and proxy statement that received ample attention in the press and from nonprofit organizations. The spin on the news about the new Foundation was intended to balance out some of the downside news concerning Easton Company revenue losses and job reductions in the region. Pratt-Miles hoped it would be perceived as a goodwill gesture to the northern Virginia community located halfway across the country from its own corporate headquarters and circle of philanthropic concerns.

George Miles was quoted saying, "The Easton Company Foundation will continue Ed Easton's philanthropic mission."

PART FIVE

THE DAY THE MERGER CLOSED

Founder's Tears From Heaven

Friday the thirteenth of November. Rain poured down. The sky turned black. The weather was the antithesis of that sunny day in August when the world learned The Easton Company's time was almost up. Clocks had been turned back from daylight savings time two weeks earlier and days were getting depressingly short On the day the merger was scheduled to close, the weather matched the mood of the Friends of The Easton Company. After months of claiming that news of the merger was enough to make Ed Easton roll over in his grave, now the Friends could claim the raindrops were Ed's tears from heaven.

For some Easton employees, getting out of bed on this day was agonizing. They dreaded the end of the Easton era. Although few knew what to expect once the day ended, most were sure it wouldn't be good. Kate Cooper dreaded this day because of the long list of human resources transactions that had to be processed and confirmed, without exception, before the merger closed.

In the human resources, finance, legal and accounting divisions, the day was already in fast-forward having never actually ended from the night before. The division heads in these areas were not going anywhere until the close was official. It did not matter that their change in control group peers were already packing. The associate division heads in these areas – one layer down from the change in control group – had been instructed to keep their cell and office phone lines open in anticipation of information requests from the close meeting in New York.

Critical support staff was told to be in the office by 7 a.m., no excuses. If your kids were sick, bring them with you. If your car broke down, someone would come pick you up. If you were delirious from fever, you would have to be ill at work. There were piles of last minute documents that required

139

approval and signatures; confirming phone calls to be made and faxes to be sent; accounts to close and funds to transfer; ending balances to report and hundreds of data points to calculate, validate and transmit to vendors, administrators, banks, lawyers, the IRS, the SEC and of course, the soon-to-be new owner, Pratt-Miles.

Pink Slips and Parting Gifts

It was the last day The Easton Company stock traded on Wall Street. The important activity, however, was taking place in the merger law firm's New York offices and the Easton headquarters building in Virginia. While the attorneys for both sides were digging through piles of company papers, Easton employees were digging though mounds of company paraphernalia. The marketing department had unlocked their storage closets and hauled out all The Easton Company wear, gifts and tchotchkes. Each item sported the soon-to-be-defunct company logo. Huge cardboard boxes of the stuff had been deposited in the atrium for employees to help themselves. It resembled the jetsam from a sinking ship.

All these goodies were leftovers from the freebies and giveaways handed out at employee meetings, or given as mementos to clients and customers. Some boxes were full and newly opened, probably secured for some future event that would now never take place. Other boxes contained remainders from past company functions: T-shirts, windbreakers, sweatshirts, coffee mugs, key chains, expensive pens, leather business card holders, paper weights, aprons, golf balls, stuffed animals, umbrellas, thermoses, carry-on bags, lanyards, sun visors, golf hats, leather portfolios, desk sets, note cubes, golf towels.

As human resources director Kate Cooper cut through the atrium to deliver an original signed release to the legal department, she couldn't help but shake her head. The scene reminded her of modern art installations she had recently seen at the Hirshhorn. This would have fit right in, she thought. We could label it Corporation Spilling Its Guts.

Weeks later, after all the stuff had been cleaned out, there were conversations about what this junk might be worth someday on eBay. But on the day of close, employees' inclination to pick up a few items from the boxes was motivated by the desire to hold on to a piece of personal history that was quickly and unbelievably ending right before their eyes.

On that last morning most Easton headquarters employees still had no idea how much longer they would have jobs. Insecurity ran rampant around the building, with the exception of the corner offices where the company's top talent was packing up for their grand exit. The merger agreement required the change in control group to leave the premises on the day of the close, their employment and access to the building terminated. These senior executives and division heads had their own cardboard boxes they were filling, but not with corporate giveaways. Their mementos included crucial files and contact lists, a few framed family photos, and visions of golden parachutes dancing through their heads.

Outside the rain poured down in sheets so heavy it sounded tropical – the weather was depressing the masses, but the corner office occupants were packing as though headed for the grandest vacations of their lives. Nothing could dampen their moods.

The previous evening, word spread among the change in control group that the deal was expected to close quickly the next morning, certainly no later than noon. But when news came from New York that the parties were breaking for lunch, most of the executives were too antsy to stick around the headquarters building any longer. A few had received a call or two with questions from the closing meeting underway at the law firm, but generally the change in control group members were unoccupied and weary of watching the nervous underlings around them.

By 1 p.m. most of the corner office occupants had departed, boxes and laptops in hand, with instructions to their secretaries to forward any calls from New York to their cell phones. Few had said any real good-byes. Most had stopped briefly at the office doors of their direct reports to offer up a crooked smile and a farewell greeting of "Good luck," or "Well, I guess this is it." Clearly these were not individuals who were interested in reminiscing or lengthy farewells.

At 2 p.m. the merger deal still had not closed in New York. But at that hour, 245 miles away in Virginia, representatives from Pratt-Miles' Human Capital group entered the Easton headquarters building and began knocking on office doors. Sitting down briefly, the reps explained to selected employees that their services would no longer be needed after today. Before mid-afternoon nearly forty Easton headquarters employees had been handed their immediate walking papers. Many were long-service employees who had worked at Easton for twenty years or more. Many had grown up there, grown wiser there, grown gray there. They had walked through Easton's front doors thousands of times – but when they walked out of the building on that Friday the thirteenth, they would never return again as employees.

Conveniently, the majority of the division heads left the building just before their long-time assistants received pink slips. Those who had read the merger proxy knew this was likely to be someone's fate. The proxy contained plenty of enhanced severance pay and benefits provisions for "our employees who are involuntarily terminated without cause before year end." Yet in such situations there exists a reality gap between knowing something is going to happen, and realizing that it's going to happen to you. For the average employee the time between the merger announcement in August and this day in November had accelerated exponentially. Then the day of the close arrived and every part of it seemed entirely surreal. In retrospect, some described the day as dreamlike, but for those long-service individuals who were handed letters of termination by someone they had never met before, it was more like a nightmare.

Elvis Has Left the Building

Bing Sullivan roared into The Easton Company parking lot on a custom Hurricane – the fastest, loudest bike in his collection. He arrived in the rain, parked under the portico at the front of the building, stowed his poncho and grabbed his bags. It was just before lunch on the day of the close, a perfect time to make an entrance.

Striding through the lobby, Bing was already in character, smiling and nodding at the receptionist and a handful of other employees who were looking at him, mouths agape. Earlier that morning, Easton's senior vice president of marketing had spent an hour with a make-up artist he had hired to help get him ready. Now his boots were making a wonderful clomp clomp sound on the polished hardwood floors, causing everyone to turn and stare. The white leather fringe swished and the rhinestones glittered as he moved through the reception area. Bing walked straight into the atrium and put down his two bags. From the first bag he quickly extracted the small battery-operated Fender amplifier and microphone, plugged in and turned on. When he arrived, people were clustered in the atrium sifting through an assortment of cardboard boxes. Others were stepping out of their offices to see what the buzz was about.

"Thank you. Thank you very much," he intoned into the mike as he adjusted the volume and bass settings. A small titter of laughter bounced through the gathering as he noticed a few more heads looking over the railing from the balcony above. "I sincerely appreciate y'all comin' out tonight. And before I go, I want to sing you one last song."

People were chuckling. Behind his sunglasses, Bing was sure most of them had no idea who he was, which was how he'd like to keep it for the moment. He hadn't spotted his secretary yet, which was a good thing. She would likely be the first to figure out it was Bing in the Elvis regalia and spread the word.

Her office was two floors up. He was counting on that distance to buy him some time to remain anonymous.

"I had a really, really hard time decidin' on what song to leave y'all with – I thought about doin' 'All Shook Up' or," he paused to let the laughter subside, "or maybe 'It's Now or Never.'"

More people were coming down the stairs.

"Of course I considered 'There Goes My Everything' and even 'Don't Be Cruel.'" Bing leaned down to start the recorded accompaniment. "But in the end, it just had to be this one." And with that, Bing launched into his winning Elvis impression:

"Well it's one for the money
Two for the show
Three to get ready
Now go cat go."

Much to Bing's satisfaction, the crowd was already whooping and laughing.

"But don't you step on my blue suede shoes. Do anything that you want to do, but uh-uh Honey, lay off o' my shoes."

Now the crowd was clapping and moving and singing along. As he finished the final verse and moved to the last chorus of the Elvis hit written by Carl Perkins, it looked like Bing's performance had attracted most everyone left in the building.

"You can do anything but lay off o' my blue suede shoes.
You can do what you want just stay off o' my blue suede shoes."

Bing gave the crowd a huge bow, "Thank you. Thank you very much. Thank you."

While the group whooped and applauded, Bing quickly stuffed the mike and amp away, grabbed his bags and jumped into the nearby elevator just as the doors were opening. Before anyone knew he was really gone, he had punched the button for the top floor and headed for his office.

It only took him ten seconds to reach his corner office after leaving the elevator. There was no one in sight. Everyone was either out of the building or down in the atrium. He'd already packed and moved all his personal belongings from his office. There was just this one last thing to do.

Unzipping the second bag, Bing pulled out the larger than life-size color poster he had Kinko's make for this occasion. Using heavy-duty two-sided

145

tape, he quickly attached the three-by-six-foot tall glossy to his office door. He took just five seconds to stand back and admire his work.

Laughing, he grabbed his bags and dashed for the fire exit stairwell. Now he was cackling like a maniac, taking the stairs two at a time, but he couldn't help himself. If the building was taller I could have parasailed off the roof, he thought. Still, this was one of the best moments he'd ever had. Reaching the ground floor just nine minutes after he arrived, Bing left the building by a side exit and was back on his motorcycle in no time.

Roaring past the front entrance, someone yelled after him, "Who the hell are you?" Bing just waved.

Meanwhile, employees who had watched the show from the upstairs balcony were returning to their desks on the top floor, speculating about who had sent the Elvis impersonator. Then they saw it. There on Bing's door hung a gigantic color photo of the guy they'd just seen perform downstairs crooning into a microphone. There was no mistaking the long sideburns, gold sunglasses, diamond rings, white rhinestone leather jumpsuit and the pointy white boots. Across the bottom of the poster in big bold block letters were the words, ELVIS HAS LEFT THE BUILDING.

Dressed to Shred

Sometime after 2 p.m. on the thirteenth of November, Kate Cooper suddenly became Easton's most senior human resources executive. The "promotion" occurred by default and without ceremony in the waning hours of The Easton Company's existence. Larry Baxter left the building and Kate found herself in charge of the division's sprint to the merger finish line.

In the past, Larry Baxter had dangled promotion like the proverbial carrot on a stick whenever he sensed Kate might be exploring other career opportunities.

"I don't anticipate staying here indefinitely, you know," he would tell Kate behind closed doors. "It's not my plan to still be here running HR when I turn sixty."

As time passed, however, Kate realized Larry Baxter really didn't have any other opportunities that might tempt him away from his lucrative career at Easton. It took a merger for him to walk away from the company.

Although they had been working closely together on merger-related project requirements over the past several weeks, Larry provided no final instructions upon his departure. His last words to Kate as he passed her office door were, "Goodbye. Good luck."

By mid-afternoon, Kate stopped taking calls long enough to run next door to the coffee shop. Even though it meant streaking through the pouring rain and maneuvering around massive puddles, she desperately needed a double espresso and a few minutes breathing room. At 3 p.m. it was so dark outside the parking lot arc lights were already aglow, rimmed with blurry halos.

Her break took only minutes, but as Kate reached Easton's portico and lowered her umbrella in front of the glass doors, she stopped mid-dash to grasp the sight she was witnessing. Although the deal still had not closed, there were workmen inside removing the name "The Easton Company" from the doors and replacing those letters with "Pratt-Miles." Seeing the company's name scraped off the glass sent a jolt to Kate's heart and lungs. "This is really happening," she whispered only to herself as she stood dripping and staring. Moving past the workers, she walked through the lobby. Two men on ladders were dismantling The Easton Company logo that hung on the wall. The workers were not the usual Easton building maintenance staff. Who are these guys, Kate pondered. She laughed, realizing her thought also applied to the new owners who had the balls to change the name on the building before they actually owned it. Yeah, who are these guys, Kate wondered.

At the front desk, the receptionist said to Kate, "They're looking for you in the finance area. Something about a Rabbi Trust? You're supposed to stop by before you go back to your office."

"Lucky me," Kate replied jokingly to the receptionist. "At least they didn't track me down in the bathroom this time."

Peeling off her raincoat, she left it along with her dripping umbrella in the visitors' closet and headed for the finance department. As she turned into the hallway leading to their offices, she slowed to observe the kluge of people gathered at the end of the corridor. For such a historic moment – at least in the annals of The Easton Company – it was certainly a strange sight.

It took Kate a minute to recognize who she was seeing. Slouched and leaning with their backs and shoulders against the walls stood the company's chief operating officer, Lee Martino, and several members of the senior level finance team. Normally, these men wore conservative suits, ties, starched white dress shirts and polished shoes to work, even on casual dress days. Now here they were in rumpled golf shirts and wrinkled khakis with boat shoes and no socks. A couple of the men wore baseball caps, the visors pulled down hard. Good Lord, Kate thought. They look like they slept in those clothes. And just as she finished the thought she realized that was exactly what they had done. A few more steps and she could see the two days beard growth and the dark circles under their eyes. Everything about them looked weary.

Before she could get any closer, one of the team's administrative assistants, Nancy Andersen, stepped out of an office and said, "Oh there you are, Kate. Lindsey has a question for you. She's either in her office or at the shredder." Lindsey Gordon was the company's chief financial officer. She and Kate often collaborated on projects related to the funding of the company's qualified benefit plans. "Thanks, Nancy," Kate replied. Then in a lower voice, gesturing with a glance up the hallway she asked, "so what's going on up there?"

Nancy looked up the hallway and back at Kate. She responded quietly, "They're waiting for the final call from New York. They've all been here since around seven last night researching and answering questions coming from the final close meeting. It's been grueling. Very early this morning the team was hunting for a missing mortgage on one of the large Nevada properties. It took hours to locate. Everyone thought this whole thing would be done early in the day. Now apparently there's some serious concern they won't close today and this will drag on through the weekend and into Monday. That wasn't the plan, but if they don't wrap up soon in New York, that's exactly what will happen, and nobody on either side really wants that. So they're waiting – and trying not to fall asleep on their feet."

"Thanks for the info," Kate replied. "I'll go find Lindsey. See you later, I hope."

"God willin' and the creek don't rise," Nancy smiled, answering in her best southern Virginia twang.

As Kate slipped quickly through the exhausted group at the end of the hall with a low key "Hi. Excuse me," she felt as though she was nearly invisible. A few of the men nodded to her as she passed but no one moved or spoke a word.

Glancing past them she caught a glimpse of the senior vice president of accounting, Lauren Bradley, stepping into her corner office. At least Kate thought it was Lauren. Normally Lauren Bradley wore dress slacks and tailored shirts to work with loafers or dress flats. Her wardrobe's color pallet was exclusively shades of black, brown, gray and white. But the person Kate had just seen enter Lauren's office – who certainly looked like Lauren – was wearing a royal blue designer suit and three inch peep-toe pumps.

Just then Kate spied Lindsey Gordon. She was standing on the other side of a glass wall efficiently feeding stacks of papers through the company's industrial-sized shredder. Lindsey, Easton's brainiac chief financial officer, had the stature of a runway model. Although she was no clotheshorse, Lindsey was a stylish dresser, but seldom wore skirts. Her trousered apparel let the financial world know she was all business. But today, Lindsey was standing at the shredder in a bright white Dior dress suit and black stiletto heels. With her short white-blonde hair and slim long legs she looked stunning. Lindsey picked up the now empty box and headed back to her office, just as Lauren emerged from her office with a box of papers, headed to the shredder. Kate glanced back over her shoulder at the weary men in the hall and then at the two women in designer suits who looked amazingly fresh and energetic. The contrast was unreal. Just as weird was the fact that these two female division heads – both members of the change in control group – were still in the building and apparently doing their own shredding.

As Lindsey emerged from her office with another stack of documents for the shredder, she saw Kate.

"Ah, just the person I need to talk to. We need to put the Rabbi Trust to bed. Want to help?"

"Do I have a choice?" Kate chuckled.

"Nah. I was just being polite," Lindsey countered.

149

"Must be the glad rags," Kate grinned.

"Must be," Lindsey replied. "There's no doubt we're dressed to shred."

Easton Transportation – Fate Unknown

Jeffrey Elkins was in possession of his Hawker 800A for less than a year when the merger with Pratt-Miles closed. At the negotiation table on that final day, one of the many remaining loose ends was the fate of Easton Transportation. With more pressing pieces of the merger deal still under discussion, Easton Transportation remained far down the agenda by mid-day.

When food was delivered to the conference room during the lunch break, Jeffrey initiated a quiet conversation about the subsidiary with Pratt-Miles CEO, George Miles. Jeffrey knew George chartered planes when he needed to, but normally flew commercial first class by choice. Pratt-Miles did not own, and apparently had no interest in owning a corporate jet. So when the two men sat down to chef salads and unsweetened iced tea, Elkins proposed to his counterpart that he be permitted to personally buy outright the assets of Easton Transportation. It seemed a logical offer. Early on in the negotiations George Miles had indicated to Jeffrey during casual conversations that Pratt-Miles probably would not keep a corporate jet. But now George Miles quickly brushed Jeffrey's suggestion aside, indicating that they would "get to all that eventually." George stressed the need to focus on more critical remaining issues if they were really going to close this deal before the end of the business day.

As late afternoon rolled in and the negotiations were still unsettled, all the players at the table were nervously intent on getting done. Still, Jeffrey felt the need to raise the issue of Easton Transportation once again, this time on the record.

"With all due respect, Jeffrey," George politely responded, "let's deal with Easton Transportation separately. I promise we'll settle it together once the deal is done. We've got to get finished here and close today – it's in everyone's best interest."

151

Other meeting participants on both sides of the table indicated their agreement. The minutes of the meeting reflected that negotiations regarding the future of Easton Transportation were "set aside for further discussion after the merger closed."

As Jeffrey Elkins got up from the conference table after the closing documents were signed and they had received confirmation of final funds wired to the appropriate accounts, he turned back to address Easton's associate general counsel, Brian Hughes. "One last thing, Brian. Give Julia West a call and tell her I said: Make sure they get their pies." With those final words, the last CEO of The Easton Company left the room.

Corporate Merger Countdown

The data-keepers were in the throes of fast-paced research to answer the latest questions raised at the settlement table in New York. Every quarter hour another call came in asking for a copy of some arcane document or a different slice of cost accounting figures than those already provided during the prior three months.

At the same time, last minute questions and requests for information were coming in from Easton employees in other locations, as well as from retirees and local politicians.

For the Easton employees handling all these matters, the last forty-eight hours seemed like some crazy reality show race – Corporate Merger Countdown.

As the day progressed, the information swapping accelerated like a fast card game of Spit. By the time the merger officially closed at 4:01 p.m. ET, most of the administrative employees who had been the working cogs and gears inside the shiny merger machine found themselves hyperventilating and disoriented. It was as though the boulder they had been tirelessly pushing up the mountain for the past three months had suddenly disappeared over the top.

"Is that it?" Marcie, one of the benefit assistants in human resources asked her supervisor, Kate Cooper. Looking up from her computer screen, Marcie blinked her eyes like a moviegoer readjusting to the daylight. "Are we done?"

"For now," Kate sighed. "There'll be plenty to clean up on the other side of this come Monday morning. You know human resources work never really ends."

Marcie groaned. "It's enough to make me wish I'd been pink-slipped today."

"Careful what you wish for, Marcie. All of us will probably be gone before much longer. Come on. Let's get out of here. I understand the party started hours ago across the street at Darwin's. Apparently someone had the foresight to book the back room."

"Not me," Marcie replied. "I'm wiped."

"But you're the party girl. You'll definitely be missed if you don't show."

"All I want to do is get myself home through the Friday night traffic in this rain. Then I'm going to sit in a hot bath 'til I'm numb, eat everything chocolate that's in the house and fall into bed in a fetal position and sleep until Sunday."

Kate smiled at Marcie. She was a hard worker and a good sport. "You have a point. I must admit I'm not exactly in the mood to party."

"Any word on the fate of the retiree medical benefits?" Marcie asked.

"Not that I've heard. Larry left without any further comment. Apparently our CEO planned to raise the topic at the close table this morning. My assumption is it was either a verbal agreement previously struck between the two CEOs, or Jeffrey hoped to slide it through at the last minute to avoid lengthy discussions. But that's just my guess. Whenever I asked Larry about the status of the retiree benefits, he said Jeffrey was handling it with Pratt-Miles. I've had my share of suspicions and concerns. In all those merger negotiation calls I monitored between the two outside law firms, there was never any specific mention of Easton retiree medical benefits."

Just then Kate heard the phone in her office ring. Marcie picked the call from her own phone and handed the receiver to Kate. It was Paul Brice, the money manager for the company's 401(k) plan, calling to confirm the final valuation of plan balances in The Easton Company stock account after the close of the market. Putting Paul on hold, Kate returned to her office so that she could pull up her spreadsheets. Following some quick checking on both sides of the call, it was apparent something was amiss. Pratt-Miles had wired funds to cover the purchase of the Easton shares in the plan, but according to Paul the amount of the wire exceeded the value of the shares by nearly $23 million.

"If you ask me, that's awfully generous of them," Paul chuckled.

"Oh God," Kate groaned. "So where do we go from here, Paul?" Kate asked, squinting her eyes shut tight as she awaited his answer. She had a vision of spending another weekend in her office. Please God, she thought, I just want to go home.

"These things happen. Remember, with more than $13 billion in cash changing hands within a matter of hours, mistakes occur. But we'll get it sorted out. We'll log the discrepancy and reconcile on Monday. As long as we have agreement by Tuesday morning and the new owner doesn't ask us for three days of interest, there shouldn't be a problem." Paul sounded exhausted.

His office had been on the phone with Kate's benefits staff much of the day tracking toward the close.

"Thanks, Paul. You guys did good work today. You'd think you were Easton employees or something," Kate joked.

Paul laughed. "Yeah, well, no offense, but right now we're pretty glad we're not. And actually, you're no longer an Easton employee either. As of about forty minutes ago I believe you became an employee of Pratt-Miles."

"Gee, Paul, I thought you were my friend." Kate chuckled.

"I take it you all are headed out to celebrate? My group has decided to go to our local watering hole and have a beer in memory of our favorite client."

"Well if that's not the sweetest sentiment," Kate chided. "Actually, Marcie and I were just discussing the party that's already in high gear at the bar across the street. I think we've both just decided to pass." Kate waved and mouthed "good night" as Marcie zipped her raincoat and walked down the hall.

"Really? But Kate, it's a truly unique reason to party. You sure you want to take a pass? What could possibly be more appealing than drinking with your fellow passengers on a sinking ship?" Paul teased.

"Hmm. More appealing? I'm thinking my sweatpants and slippers, carryout Pad Thai, a bottle of Chardonnay, and a very patient husband."

"I like your style," Paul answered. "Take care. Talk to you Monday."

"You bet," said Kate and hung up the phone.

CEO Email #1 – You Say Goodbye...

On the day of the close at 3:49 p.m., reality struck home for any Easton employee who had not yet faced the fact that this merger was actually an acquisition. Those still at their desks opened and read the last internal email they would receive as employees of The Easton Company.

From: Jeffrey W. Elkins
Sent: November 13
To: All Easton Employees
Subject: Parting Message

On Wednesday, November 4, shareholders voted to approve the merger between The Easton Company and Pratt-Miles. This action by our shareholders is to be followed by the closing today, at which time I will step aside as chief executive officer. This company has enjoyed a long and memorable history as an innovator in our industry, and Easton has been known as a distinguished company in our governance, principles and integrity. The company was founded on underlying principles articulated by our late founder, Ed Easton – to do good work, reward those that invest with us, and always enhance the experiences of the employees.

The Easton Company is a unique organization and I have had the privilege of working with wonderful colleagues. Our results have been superb, and we have served the shareholder in an extraordinary way. I know the Board feels that management has articulated and executed a strategic plan that has been remarkable in its clarity and accuracy, and also, most importantly, in delivering value to shareholders.

After nearly three decades, I depart with mixed emotions, leaving behind many talented colleagues. The Easton Company has indeed been a remarkable enterprise, fundamentally committed to improving the quality of life in America wherever we do business.

I have great confidence that George Miles, Pratt-Miles CEO, will guide the combined new company to new heights. I know this will offer opportunity for the vast majority of colleagues in The Easton Company and the true legacy of the company will be its quality employees and its important projects spread across the land.

With all good wishes for your continued success,

Jeffrey W. Elkins

In the future, former Easton employees at Pratt-Miles would derisively refer to this last communication from their ex-CEO as Jeffrey's sayonara suckers email.

CEO Email #2 – I Say Hello

Twelve minutes later, at 4:01 p.m., another important email greeting slid through the electronic ether and smacked its readers like a cold wet towel.

From: Miles, George
Sent: November 13
To: All Easton Employees
Subject: Message From Your CEO

I am pleased to announce that the merger of The Easton Company with Pratt-Miles has been completed. This transaction recognizes the special values that have been built by The Easton Company since its founding.

All of us at Pratt-Miles look forward with great anticipation and excitement to melding two terrific corporations and their dedicated employees. We are about to become the most profitable and productive company in our industry, worldwide.

Please join me and members of Pratt-Miles' senior management team in the lobby of the former Easton headquarters building for coffee on Monday morning at 9 a.m. as we begin to build our future together, moving forward into an extraordinary new period of creativity, growth, profitability and trust.
Sincerely,

George Miles

The reaction of most Easton corporate employees who read George Miles' email that afternoon? Wow. We're being invited to our own place of work by the new CEO from Denver who has never before stepped foot in this building.

Gone Skiin'

After reading the emails from Jeffrey Elkins and George Miles, Fletcher Johnston heaved a sigh. He scanned the piles of never-ending legal papers that had cluttered his desk at The Easton Company for more than four decades and realized that his career at Easton had come to an end. He pushed back in his rolling chair the way a big eater might finally push back from a smorgasbord table after a huge meal. He took a celebratory swig from his Diet Coke and realized he was done...even though the work would go on and on.

After the exciting events of Fletcher Johnston's early years at Easton, the balance of his career had become relatively tedious. The work kept him constantly busy but most days it involved conference calls and meetings, reviewing land acquisition documents and legal briefs – nothing like the travel and undercover land deals that absorbed his time when Ed Easton first hired him. Over the years he mentored plenty of new young attorneys and provided quiet but critical support to the company's general counsel – a position he had turned down twice during his long career, not wanting the stress, politics or attention.

Fletcher much preferred a behind-the-scenes role. He had learned early on that job status was not really something to be coveted unless you had a big ego to feed. Oh, there had been plenty of nights when he slept on his office couch, not thinking it worth the effort to make the trip back to the condo after working late into the evening. His office had become like a second home in many ways. The razor, comb and toothbrush in his bottom desk drawer and ever-present change of clean clothes in a dry-cleaning bag on the back of his office door attested to this fact.

A confirmed bachelor (after one brief then broken engagement that brought him as close to marriage as he ever wanted to be), he still thoroughly

160

enjoyed the company of women, but not their demanding ways. He found women so much more fascinating and intellectually stimulating than men. Through his thirties and forties he made a habit of befriending the newly hired single women at Easton, often taking them on one "welcome date" but never a second, no matter how interesting or pretty they were. He was always a gentleman, always polite beyond reason. Fletcher's nickname around the office was "the oblivious heartbreaker" or "OH!" for short. In Washington society circles, his reputation as one of the most eligible bachelors in the nation's capital endured for two decades.

Fletcher stood and stretched and then shut down his computer. He had no need for it from this moment on. The files he wanted were already backed up on a far superior system in his home office. Acquiring more hardware just because it was his for the taking was not Fletcher's style. He was a minimalist who preferred the best quality in anything he chose to own.

Fletcher looked at his watch – it was nearly 4:30 p.m. – and glanced out the window where he noticed for the first time the sheets of rain coming down. So he would get wet on the walk to his car, he shrugged to himself. No matter. A baptism of sorts seemed an appropriate start to the next stage of his life's adventure, whatever that might be.

Running a hand through his short blond-going-gray hair, he turned slowly in place to take in this room one last time. It had been the stage for so many hours of his life, but there was nothing here he needed; nothing he really wanted. The observation was a refreshing relief. After tossing his office keys onto the desk, Fletcher pulled his raincoat from its hanger on the back of the door. As he did so he noticed for the first time in years the old skis planted in the corner. Fletcher chuckled to himself and then said out loud, "Oh, why not?" in his best *que sera sera* voice. Shouldering the skis, he flicked off his office light and pulled shut a locked office door behind him.

Walking down the hallway to his favorite back exit to the parking lot, one of the young paralegals noticed the vintage skis and did a double take.

"Hey Mr. Johnston – where are you going with those?"

"Peru," Fletcher intoned in his best British boarding school accent, not breaking stride toward the exit. Then glancing back at the paralegal with a devilish grin, "I understand there's some amazing skiing in the Andes." With that, the one person whose career had seen both the beginning and the end of The Easton Company quietly disappeared into the rain and fog.

161

Corporate Love in the Time of Merger

This is the story of Cindy and Rob. Once upon a time Cindy and Rob were just coworkers. Then one day they became accountants in love.

Romantic relationships at work are never easy. Theirs certainly had extra obstacles. Both Cindy and Rob worked for The Easton Company at corporate headquarters. Both were divorced and each had multiple young children living with them.

Five years before the merger was even a twinkle in Jeffrey Elkins' eye, Cindy and Rob started dating. Their love affair began innocently enough, going out to lunch together. Their lunches at local restaurants were soon replaced by drives to quiet parks or abandoned farm roads. But then tax time was upon them and no one in accounting was going out to lunch, or any other meal for that matter. With kids at home, and no time or place to be alone together, it wasn't too long before the couple threw caution to the wind.

One night, when both Cindy and Rob were working late and each had a relative babysitting their kids, they stayed on at their desks working after everyone else in the accounting division had gone home. They lingered so long, only the front desk security guard was left in the building. Rob and Cindy exchanged looks across the accounting office's sea of workstations, waiting for the bottom of the hour when the guard made his rounds.

After the guard passed through their area and they had each smiled and nodded to him to send him on his way, the pair finally consummated their relationship in the accounting conference room.

Unexpectedly, yet to no great surprise, the consummation was more successful than planned. Three weeks later Cindy discovered she was pregnant. Rob and Cindy were married at the end of tax season. They sold their two smaller houses and together with their kids moved into a larger home. The baby arrived early but healthy, bringing their collective brood total to five – all under age eleven. Once married and living under one roof, the couple still did not have the time or a place to be alone together – but they had each other.

The least complicated part of their lives was working for The Easton Company. They could go to work together, see each other during the day, and understand without question what the other person was dealing with on the job. Both were excellent accountants and enjoyed their careers. Even though Cindy and Rob were in the same division neither one reported to the other, so there was no required job change or department move when they got married. Cindy and Rob had excellent company benefits and by marrying they decreased the total cost of their health insurance, even with the addition of a new baby. Life was crazy, hectic and demanding, but life for Cindy and Rob was better than either had experienced before.

Five years later with their youngest child in nursery school, and their oldest just starting high school, Cindy and Rob were finally able to glance up from the demands of home, kids and work, and get out to a movie by themselves now and then. Optimistically, they had even restarted home delivery of a morning newspaper with the idea that they might at last have time to read one.

The entire family had just returned from a week at the beach. This was their first vacation where all the kids had gotten along well together. No one sulked. There were no major blow-ups, and they entertained each other with cards, games, impromptu excursions, and good old playing on the beach activities. The week had been full of laughter and silliness. Their miniature golf outing had been a huge success – the most fun and chaos the seven of them had ever experienced together as a group. No one whined about who got what color ball or who went first, and there was no trip to the local emergency room to stitch up one child's forehead from another one's unanticipated backswing. The kids had come home from vacation in good spirits and Cindy and Rob returned to work feeling less stressed than when they left. School would be starting up again in a few weeks. Life was feeling pretty good to Cindy and Rob.

The next Friday the company announced its plans to merge with Pratt-Miles. Fearful worry consumed Cindy and Rob. The possibility that both their jobs could be eliminated within days, weeks or months of each other put them in double jeopardy. Each began to search for a new employer. The stress level at work, at home, in the car, and in bed was off the charts.

On the rainy Friday the merger closed, Cindy was among the first group of Easton employees laid off by Pratt-Miles. She was summoned to meet with a Pratt-Miles representative she had never seen before who politely told her she should gather her personal belongings and be gone by the end of the workday. Her services were no longer needed. Then he collected her keys, codes, and her company swipe ID that provided after hours access into the headquarters building. No further explanation was given – no one seemed to think more information was necessary, even for a solid worker like Cindy who had been employed by The Easton Company since graduating from college.

Distraught, Cindy returned to her cubicle. Rob was not at his desk. The thought that he might also be asked to leave by the end of the day made her feel short of breath. So many emotions raced though her body and brain at the same time, she could hardly bear it. How is this happening? Why is this happening?Those thoughts kept looping though her consciousness as she sat at her desk trying to focus. How could she be expected to pack fifteen years of her work life into a cardboard box in ninety minutes?

Cindy was crying quietly and gathering the family photos and other office knick-knacks from her shelf when Rob returned to his desk on the other side of the open office space. He took one look at his wife and guessed what had happened. He was also aware that their personal life was playing out in front of many sets of watchful eyes in accounting. Rob dropped the files from his meeting onto his desk and quickly walked to his wife's cubicle.

"You?" she looked at him and asked.

"No. Not yet anyway. Here, let's walk out to the car so we can talk. I'll carry that," Rob said, picking up the box she had been filling.

Following a fifteen-minute conversation in the parking lot, Rob went back to his desk and Cindy headed across the street to Darwin's where the merger party was getting underway. Rob told her he would meet her there within the hour.

She had downed multiple Molsons by the time Rob joined her at the bar. He sidled among the gathering crowd of Easton employees to stand next to Cindy, who had arrived early enough to snag a good seat. Looking around the room, clearly she was not the only one attempting to kill the pain of rejection by his new employer.

The good news was that Rob was still employed – at least for the moment. There was already talk of more layoffs coming before year-end, so the timeline on job security was anyone's guess.

Rob ordered a beer. "I called the kids already and told them we'd be home later, but before bedtime. I gave Kelly permission to order pizza and put her in charge until we get home."

"Good idea," Cindy mumbled, her eyes glazed and staring off into space.

"Hey, you OK? I mean, you're going to be OK, you know. You'll find another job. Everything will all sort itself out eventually." Rob draped his arm around her shoulder as he talked.

"Easy for you to say," she answered with a definite edge to her voice.

"I know you're angry..."

"And hurt, and confused, and pissed off, and shocked and a whole lot of other things I haven't figured out yet."

"And drunk?" Rob smiled at her.

Not anticipating Rob's comment, Cindy got caught drinking and laughing at the same time.

"Not fair." she finally managed, blotting her mouth after getting control of herself again.

"Look, I have to be honest with you here. I thought you would go first. After all, you got hired six years after I did." Cindy gave her husband a look he was quite familiar with – the one that showed up along with many of her feminist observations.

"Oh, and what? You think they laid you off first because I'm a guy and you're not?"

"More likely because you're the higher paid breadwinner and I'm just the working wife."

"Wait a minute. Am I getting blamed for this? How is this my fault? The good news is that as of right now at least one of us still has a job."

Cindy and Rob each took another pull on their beers and surveyed the room, letting their emotions settle before continuing.

"No, not your fault," Cindy said in a calmer voice. "But I've got some bad news for you."

"What's that?"

In a slow and measured tone Cindy replied, "I really hate your new employer," and again Cindy melted into laughter. Rob couldn't help but laugh with her.

"OK. My work here is done," Cindy announced, sliding off the bar stool she'd been occupying.

"Wait. I was planning to have another beer and talk to some of the guys," Rob replied.

"Not a problem. Take my seat. I'll meet you at the car in a bit."

"Where are you going?"

"Back to my desk. There're a couple things I forgot to get."

"Bad idea Cindy. Seriously, hold up. You can't go back in. They made that clear. Anyway, you don't have your swipe card anymore," Rob pointed out as he reached for his second beer.

"True," Cindy answered, "but I have yours," she grinned, holding up his company ID and backing away from him toward the door.

"Hey. Bring that back. Anything you left I can get for you on Monday. I'm not kidding. You don't want to get us both fired, do you?"

"Don't worry. I promise I'll behave. After fifteen years I need one last look around before I take my leave."

"Meet me at the car in thirty minutes, Cindy." He caught her eye and gave her a stern look. "And don't get yourself killed crossing the street."

Cindy threw her husband an air kiss and gave him a little wave with his swipe card as she left the bar.

Cindy entered the Easton building for the last time using her husband's swipe at the back door so she wouldn't need to pass the security guard at the front desk. Once inside, she stood for a minute and listened. The building was quiet. Ex-Easton employees had either gone home or decamped to Darwin's. Pratt-Miles interlopers were already headed for the airport.

Cindy boarded the freight elevator at the back of the building and rode it to the top floor. Stepping out into the quiet darkness was eerie. The lights were already dimmed for the evening and the conference rooms and desks were all empty.

"What does this remind me of?" she kept asking herself. She wasn't sure, but it definitely no longer felt like her workplace.

Using the wide-open stairs in the middle of the atrium, she continued to make a quick floor-by-floor tour as a final farewell to a place that had been her life for so long. When she reached her cubicle, she pulled out the bottom drawer of her desk as far as it would go. Then she leaned down and reached deep into the opening where she had long ago duct-taped a No. 10 envelope. Inside was $200 cash emergency money – an amount that had seemed like a small fortune when she put it there years ago right after she and Rob started dating. Also in the envelope was a condom two pack – just in case. Added to the envelope after discovering she was pregnant, Cindy recalled thinking that one conception at work was enough.

After slipping the envelope securely into her purse, Cindy stepped to the window overlooking the parking lot to see if Rob was waiting for her at the car. She was glad there was no sign of him yet. I have a few more minutes before I have to walk out the door, she thought. Although Rob wasn't in the parking lot, she did notice the young weekend security guard was out there, leaning into a car window, apparently talking to friends.

Cindy retraced her steps to the center of the atrium where the space at the core of the building opened three stories above. You could stand there next to the stairs and look all the way up through the glass pyramids on the roof. It was a special place in the building – it was, after all, designed by an architectural genius.

Cindy stood in that spot looking up, her hands clutched to her chest and swaying slightly. Her eyes glistened with emotion. She recalled all the good things that had happened to her in this place, under this roof. Tears ran down her face. It didn't seem so long ago that she was bringing the baby to work to show him off to friends and coworkers before returning from leave. The baby had gotten hungry and began crying before she could take him out to the car and feed him. She remembered how his cries had echoed when she walked through this open space. Now she was the one crying. She was crying the way women cry when they are intensely angry. With her fists and eyes clenched tight and tears streaming, Cindy screamed in the loudest voice she had ever used, "Damn you Jeffrey Elkins!"

A Toast to Ed

It was just past midnight and still drizzling when Ben, Jack, Rita, Liz and Patti tumbled out of Darwin's.

"Who's driving?" Jack asked the group.

"Whoever's got the most years of service," Rita replied.

"That would be me," said Patti. "I worked at Easton for nineteen years and four months."

"Maybe that should be whoever has the longest service and is the most sober," Jack amended.

"Oh how soon they forget," Ben added as they huddled under the pub's awning. "I have nineteen years and six months, Liz. Don't you recall I was on the interview panel when you were hired?" Ben pulled out his keys and the group headed for Ben's Jeep Cherokee.

"So Liz – you sure you know where we're going and how to get there?" Ben asked, his fingers on the ignition key as his passengers pulled their doors shut.

"Sure. I mean, I know how to get to the entrance, and it's relatively small, so I'm certain we can find it if you actually have a flashlight," Liz answered leaning forward from the back seat.

Rita opened the glove compartment and pulled out a large Maglite. She pushed the switch twice watching the torch flash on and off again. "Looks like we're good in that department," she noted.

"And in my handbag I've got the glasses Jack borrowed from the bar, along with the open bottle of Hennessy the bartender gave me, breaking God knows how many Virginia ABC laws," Patti giggled.

"Yeah, you got the brandy and he got your phone number," Rita chuckled. "Apparently he decided you were worth the risk."

"He must have decided there was no chance you were an undercover cop," Ben added.

"So are you okay to drive Ben?" Jack asked. "We can sit here for a bit and make Liz draw us a map in case she's so drunk she falls asleep before we get there."

"Am not," Liz insisted in a defiant but slightly slurred voice.

"Yeah, I'm good," Ben said starting the SUV. "Let's go before it starts raining hard again or we get too tired and change our minds."

Twenty minutes later Ben and the rest of the group stood in a semicircle around a marble headstone in a small cemetery. The rain had stopped but the sky was still overcast. The darkness was disrupted only by the diffused yellow beams from the fog lights on the parked Jeep and Ben's flashlight sitting in the wet grass illuminating the grave marker.

"Okay, let's do this," said Jack in an uneasy voice.

"What's wrong, Jack? Scared of ghosts?" Patti mewed.

"Not particularly. Although I have to admit this is a bit creepier than I anticipated. Actually, I'm more concerned about a police car gliding by and seeing lights in here. Given our alcohol consumption this evening, I doubt it would be a particularly pleasant encounter."

"Understood," answered Ben, as he reached into Patti's large leather purse and started distributing glasses.

"I'll do that," Jack said, reaching over to take the Hennessy bottle from Patti's less than steady hand. After pouring everyone a double, Jack faced the tombstone raising his glass and the others did the same. "To Ed!" Jack stated in a firm and steady voice that caught even him by surprise.

"To Ed!" the others echoed.

"Thanks, Ed," Patti whispered. "It was a truly fine company."

"To all those good years, Ed," Ben raised his glass.

"To the good years!" the group caroled back.

"We'll remember you, Ed – even though it's not The Easton Company anymore..." Liz broke off with a sob.

As they drained their glasses the rain picked up again. Jack tipped the brandy bottle and poured the rest of its contents onto Ed Easton's grave. "Truly glad you weren't here to see it all end, Ed," Jack mumbled as he nestled the sophisticated empty, label facing out, into the grass next to the headstone. The others were already making their way back to the Jeep. "A proud moment it's not. But it was a damn good company while it lasted." Jack picked up the flashlight and shone it on Ed Easton's epitaph:

Dreams become reality when people believe and act together

The $2,300 Bar Tab

If the walls in Darwin's Bar and Grille could talk, they could tell the oral history of Easton's rise and fall. It would include the juiciest tales from The Easton Company story. Darwin's had opened across the street within months after the first employees moved into Easton's headquarters building – back in the days when there was nothing else across the street except graded mud, survey markers and the promise of a community yet to be built. At first out of necessity, and later owing to corporate culture and tradition, Darwin's was the de facto company cafeteria for the lifespan of the corporation: the primary watering hole, lunch and dinner venue, offsite interview spot, corporate secret-sharing scene and rant-rage, gut-spilling location.

So the place for the post-sale, post-mortem party was never in question. The early adapters had arrived on site and ordered a first round soon after the initial pink slip meetings were ending. But the bulk of attendees started streaming across the street through the rain sometime shortly after 4 p.m. when cell phone calls between the bar and the offices confirmed that the back room at Darwin's had been reserved and a bar tab was already running.

By 4:30 the crowd in Darwin's back room was thick with new arrivals mixed with those whose blood alcohol levels already reflected a good three hours of drinking. No one was leaving. There was too much to discuss and rehash. Too much disbelief to wash away. In another setting or another locale the bartenders would have been more vigilant. But everyone in Darwin's – customer and employee – knew this was the end of an era playing out. Car keys would be confiscated or voluntarily handed over before the night's end; cabs would be called and rides would be given, but no one would be cut off or tossed out. Not even when the flaming tequilas were ordered just before midnight.

Long past the early rounds of limed Coronas and well into the throes of mojitos, lemondrops and chocolate martinis, someone thought to order a few trays of appetizers: dips and bites that provided no real sustenance for the growing crowd, just something to absorb a small portion of the alcohol and keep people on their feet.

Amazingly those in attendance in Darwin's back room included a few well-liked members of the change in control group, a number of the remaining high-level executives, and dozens of Easton's rank-and-file employees. With more than 150 people crammed into the private party venue, only a few souls thought to ask who was paying for all this.

As the night grew late and some partygoers attempted to pay and leave, the bartenders just shook their heads and smiled saying, "It's been taken care of. Do you have a ride? Need a taxi?" But no one asked who was paying – too inebriated or grateful, they simply took the news at face value.

A small group of mournful revelers leaving Darwin's just before 10 p.m. were still sober enough to notice the crane parked across the street in front of the headquarters building. They stood and stared as the hoist ripped from the ground the thirty-year-old copper and concrete sign that read *The Easton Company* and dropped it like so much scrap into a waiting dump truck.

Just before 2 a.m., the last nonpaying customer departed Darwin's private room after saying goodnight to the one remaining bartender and to Jody Glick, now former vice president of Easton Company specialty marketing. Brad the bartender smoothly moved down to the far end of the bar where Jody had held court all evening. Brad and Jody were old friends. He grinned as he poured a last shot of Glenfiddich into Jody's nearly empty glass.

"Thanks, Brad."

"You're welcome Jody. You are one amazing person, you know that? Lots of folks worth more money than you drank here tonight and it never crossed their minds to open their wallets."

"Life's been good to me. Anyway, they don't know what they're missing."

"So where's the thrill?"

Jody tipped back the contents from her scotch tumbler and stubbed out the illegally smoked cigarette in the saucer Brad had slipped her ten minutes earlier. "The thrill, my friend, is in being anonymously generous. The people here tonight – and a number of people who will wish they *had* been here tonight – will be talking about this last Easton bash for years to come. In the morning, a few will wake up and think to ask, 'Who picked up the tab last night?'"

"You mean wake up this afternoon?"

"Right," Jody chuckled. "This afternoon."

"And no one will ever know?" Brad asked, confirming the instructions Jody had given him earlier in the day.

"Correct. This is our little secret."

"Okay then. Ready to total up what your happy little secret is going to set you back?"

"Sure."

Brad walked to the register and ran the grand total. "Just over twenty-three hundred."

"Worth every penny. What about the taxis?"

"The taxi company agreed to bill you directly."

"You are good, my man Brad. Thanks for all your help tonight," Jody winked as she handed him her personal AmEx gold card.

"My pleasure. I'll play Little John to your Robin Hood any day."

PART SIX

UNDER NEW MANAGEMENT

In the News

Two days after the sale of The Easton Company concluded, the business sections of the Sunday city newspapers were filled with commentary, letters to the editors and an assortment of stories about "the most significant commercial real estate deal in North America since the Indians sold Manhattan." One reporter chose to speculate on Ed Easton's beyond-the-grave reaction to the sale of his company.

November 15
The *Sunday Record*
What Would Ed Have Said?

Ed Easton's philosophy for the company he founded put the bottom line at the bottom of the list of corporate priorities.

But that approach disappeared from The Easton Company's management strategy years ago. Now Easton's name will also disappear.
As the purchase by Pratt-Miles was concluded on Friday with billions of dollars changing hands, The Easton Company followed the trajectory of many U.S.-based corporations. It was started by an entrepreneur, built up with his guidance and then went into its second act with a new set of management. Now it's being sold to a larger company as the industry consolidates.

On numerous occasions before his death several years ago, Ed Easton maintained the purpose of setting up The Easton Company was to serve human needs. If done correctly, he said, profits would follow, but to Ed Easton profit was secondary.

The company went public in 1966. It turned a large portion of northern Virginia farmland into one of the earliest and most successful planned communities in the nation. It later created some of the most unusual and successful urban redevelopment projects in the country, which accelerated inner-city revitalization in numerous U.S. cities.

As the company progressed, it focused more on ownership and acquisition. It continued growing its land development business with communities west of the Rockies, concentrating on Las Vegas and San Diego.

Profits soared. The company brought in $1.1 billion last year. Final evidence of its growth came Friday when the deal with Pratt-Miles concluded with the new owner paying a thirty-three percent premium over Easton's closing price on the day before the sale was announced in August.

Ed Easton's philanthropic energies have been well documented. So what would Easton have thought about the sale of the company he founded and nurtured to prominence?

"It's an incredible hypothetical, but after he retired he was very respectful of the way the new leadership needed to take on situations," said a former Easton vice president who declined to be named for this article. "He was constantly changing with the times. He saw life as a set of opportunities."

"Current executives have acted responsibly in managing the company. Even as they agreed to the sale, Easton Chief Executive Officer Jeffrey Elkins insisted on establishing and fully funding The Easton Foundation."

Plans are to channel about $4 million in charitable donations through the Foundation each year. The bulk of those donations will go to a variety of organizations, such as a $100,000 pledge to the Virginia Museum of Modern Art, $80,000 to NOVA-Health Medical Center, and a $60,000 donation to the Virginia Symphony Orchestra.

The Foundation did not return calls for comment.

Elkins got an extraordinary price for shareholders and he was able to ensure that The Easton Foundation will carry on good works in the community into the future. The Foundation's work in Virginia and around the metro region will no doubt preserve Ed Easton's legacy.

Few readers knew that Jeffrey Elkins' new personal press secretary wrote this editorial-like news article. It was only after the merger was consummated that stockholders and the public learned that Jeffrey had conveniently named himself The Easton Foundation's chairman. What wasn't reported was that the millions of dollars Elkins had secured for the Foundation – along with his six figure salary, a very nice office with a northwest D.C. address, and an executive secretary of his own choosing – had come from the proceeds of the sale, not from the new owner. Or as some perceived it, out of the pockets of the stockholders and the company's retirees.

Easton No More

The line of former Easton corporate employees snaked in through the front doors of their workplace at precisely 9 a.m. Monday morning. Most were dressed to impress. George Miles was there with a big smile to greet each person, introduce himself and shake hands. It was like meeting the new minister of the church you'd been attending since childhood.

Once through the reception line, people quietly milled around the table of pastries and coffee set out on silver service and white linen. Those choosing to talk were muttering softly and standing close. Animated conversations and laughter – the hallmarks of Easton Company gatherings – were noticeably absent.

The sophisticated three-dimensional Easton Company logo, which hung in the headquarters lobby for years, had been replaced by Pratt-Miles' gaudy and cartoonish orange logo. People stayed long enough to be polite, but once assured that there would be no speeches or other announcements from the new management, they drifted away to their offices.

The morning reception felt freshly artificial to employees as they passed the now empty offices of senior management and the desks of nearly fifty coworkers who had been pink-slipped just three days earlier. Some offices were starkly vacant. Others looked as though the occupants had evacuated in the face of a natural disaster.

Before leaving the lobby, each employee was encouraged to take a small gift from their new employer: a coffee mug filled with orange jelly beans and imprinted with the Pratt-Miles logo and slogan, *Pratt-Miles – You're Gonna Love Us!*

Monday Morning Hangover – The $22 Million Error

Kate left the morning reception holding only a slim portfolio and walked toward what had been the offices of Easton corporate finance. Before leaving her office on Friday, she had hastily scheduled a meeting with her counterparts in accounting and finance. With all three of their division heads gone, Glen, the senior director of finance, Greta, the managing director of accounting, and Kate, the human resources director, were now in charge of the remains. It was up to them to initiate the call to Pratt-Miles headquarters in Denver to resolve the $22 million transfer error made at the close on Friday afternoon – an error of which Pratt-Miles management was apparently still unaware.

Greta and Kate walked into Glen's office together and Glen quietly closed the door. No one took a seat. Somehow the idea of having this conversation standing up, leaning against walls and furniture, seemed less serious. Or maybe it was the pretense that if they remained standing, this issue really wouldn't take as long or be as critical as it sounded.

Glen sighed. "So. Exactly what are we looking at here?" He and Greta both stared at Kate.

Kate reached into her portfolio and pulled out a single piece of paper containing less than a half page of print. It was the confirmation email from the 401(k) plan administrator verifying that when Pratt-Miles wired funds to cover the purchase of the Easton shares in the plan, the amount of the wire exceeded the value of the shares by nearly $23 million. It took just ninety seconds to read the text of the email out loud from start to finish.

"For the love of Pete," Greta exclaimed. "I've been saying for weeks the Pratt-Miles accounting group in Denver were idiots. They couldn't even get the fund transfer right."

179

"We walked them through these figures enough times. I'm just not clear on how they arrived at a transfer amount that is $22,664,475 more than the stock price we needed to cover. Any ideas about what that additional number might represent?" Kate asked hopefully looking at the other two.

"Not a clue," Glen replied shaking his head. "I was helping search for the missing mortgage and lease documents for La Vista Place on Friday. How the heck someone misplaces that kind of paperwork for a 700-acre development project worth more than a hundred million is beyond me. Anyway, that's my excuse for being useless on this one."

"What's that number again?" Greta asked.

"$22,664,475" Kate replied.

"Let me get something from my office. It sounds vaguely familiar but I'm not placing the source. I'll be right back." Greta opened the door and stepped out of the office.

"How are you holding up?" Kate asked Glen, taking a look at the exhaustion showing on his face that no doubt mirrored the dark circles under her own eyes.

"Oh, well. You know." Glen dipped his head to one side while shrugging his shoulders and rolling his eyes. "I sense this is only the beginning of the end. Do you think you'll be staying?" he asked gingerly.

"Not for long. Not likely anyway. The senior human resources executive in Denver has already suggested I might want to start looking for another job." Kate chuckled bleakly. "Like I don't see the writing on the wall. Especially after telling them I wasn't interested in moving to Denver. Not that saying yes would have made a difference. The reality is that I'm more experienced and higher paid than their most senior human resources executive. It seems they are either threatened by me or afraid of me. Mostly they don't know how to react to the straightforward answers and information I keep giving them. On conference calls with the Denver team there's always several seconds of dead silence after I respond to whatever they're asking about. Half the time I can't figure out if they have no idea what I'm talking about or if they're pondering the veracity of my reply. It's weird. I'd give anything to have them on a video call so I could see their faces and assess their reactions."

"What do you think their reaction will be to this?" Glen asked nodding toward the paper Kate was still holding in her hand.

"Clueless. Part of me thinks the three of us could take the $22 million, transfer it to an offshore account and they'd never miss it. Not that I'm suggesting that. Just commenting on Denver's apparent lack of math skills, or whatever you want to attribute this screw-up to." As Greta walked back in Kate finished, "This isn't our mistake, that's for sure. This is a Pratt-Miles blunder."

"Amen to that," Greta chimed in. "I found what I was looking for. Those idiots in Pratt-Miles corporate accounting failed to follow our simple instructions about how to handle the restricted Easton shares. The $22 million? That's the gross value of the restricted shares held by Easton executives along with the related tax withholdings owed. Now the money for those shares and the taxes appear to have been moved into the Easton Company Rabbi Trust. It wasn't part of the merger plan or anyone's intention for those funds to actually go into the Rabbi Trust at close. But it looks like that's what happened. Of course Pratt-Miles hasn't named new trustees yet for any of the Easton plans, which means the named trustees for the Rabbi Trust whose signatures we would need to fix this mess are all former Easton executives. And none of them can legally initiate a reversal to pull the erroneous deposit of funds back out of the Trust."

"Oh great," Kate moaned. "Now we'll face the legal question about a distribution from the Rabbi Trust to fix an erroneous contribution to an executive retirement plan upon merger. Shoot me now."

"You've gotta wonder how these people tie their shoes and start their cars in the morning." Greta enthused.

For a moment there was quiet in the room. Glen had been staring at a coffee stain on the green carpet that was left like a birthmark in his office during the closing melee Friday afternoon. He was feeling the same frustration and superiority being voiced by these two very bright women – they were much smarter than most of the men he worked with, but he would never admit that out loud. Yet even smart women let their emotions cloud the reality of the moment. He was being quiet, waiting to see if Kate and Greta would realize what had suddenly struck him hard in the gut a few minutes earlier when both women asserted their fiercest "us versus them" posturing that this was a Pratt-Miles error.

Glen glanced up and saw the two women staring at him with looks of concern and expectation on their faces – an expression of emotions rarely found on the faces of most men he knew and worked with.

"What is it, Glen?" Greta asked. "What are we missing here?"

Kate added, "Yeah, what are you thinking over there. I get the feeling you're somehow a few steps ahead of us on this. You have that look on your face."

That made Glen give a little guffaw from behind the hand that was now stretched across his forehead. Apparently his lack of emotion had given him away.

"Well," Glen stretched the word out and paused for another one of his large sighs, "it's just this. Like it or not – no matter what occurred before today – as of this morning it's no long us versus them. Starting today, their problems are now our problems. Their errors are our errors."

"Thanks Glen," Kate said. "I guess we had that coming."

"Despite the fact that you are dead-on accurate as usual Glen," Greta retorted, "it still doesn't make me like your perspective."

"However," Kate grinned impishly, "since Greta and I need to go look in the mirror for a bit and practice our best we-are-now-Pratt-Miles smiles and pronoun usage, how about you initiate the call to Denver on this one? We'll be available if you need back up." Kate extended her arm holding the printed email message toward Glen as she snapped shut her portfolio with the other hand.

"Nice try, gorgeous," Glen laughed. "I wasn't trying to be a smart-ass. I was just saying the dividing line is gone. The tug of war is over and we got pulled across to the other side. So it's time to drop the rope and..."

"Get on the bus?" Greta interrupted.

"Drink the Kool-Aid?" Kate said in a singsong voice. "Greta, go get this man a mug of orange jelly beans from the lobby. He's definitely on board."

"Okay, okay. You made your point. And yes, I'll even make the call, but not without the two of you in the room. So I guess we'd better sit down and walk through what we need to say to our friends in Denver before it gets to be 8 a.m. mountain time."

"Maybe there is some good news in this 'we're all Pratt-Miles now' perspective after all," Kate said as she moved to sit down.

"Yeah, what's that?" Greta asked, also taking a seat.

Looking back at Glen she continued, "It just occurred to me that the people ultimately responsible for resolving this thing are no longer in this building. Our bosses and the Easton decision-makers are gone and no one else in the Pratt-Miles organization is even aware of it. Under the circumstances, it's not as though anyone has actually asked us to take charge of anything yet. To put it another way, I don't think the fix on this one is in our court. So although we'll be supplying them the information, the reconciliation work on this particular mess is likely to take place in Denver, not here. Good news friends. When we hang up the phone at the end of the call, this problem will be out of our hands. We're resource, but we're no longer corporate. Right Glen?"

"Right Kate. Which is why I'm willing to make the call."

"Suddenly I feel a lot lighter. If this is what being relieved of responsibility feels like, I may enjoy learning to live with it," Greta chuckled.

"All right guys, let's get through this and I'll buy the coffee when we're done," Kate offered.

With another huge sigh, Glen pushed the door closed again so the three former Easton employees could strategize in private their presentation of facts regarding the $22 million Pratt-Miles error.

Twenty-First-Century Corporate Sampler

Soon after Easton headquarters became a Pratt-Miles regional office, Phyllis Simpson took down the ten-year-old framed photo over her desk. The photo captured the joy on her face as Ed Easton congratulated her for twenty years of company service. She was now just one of five remaining secretaries who had been employed at Easton headquarters. All the others were laid off.

In place of the photo, Phyllis hung a newly completed cross-stitched sampler she had made following the merger. Captured in a slim gold frame, the bold block maroon letters read:

WE MUST COME TO AN END

ABOUT WHAT USED TO BE

NO LONGER COMPANY A

WE ARE NOW COMPANY B

In the News

December 15
The *Washington Scene* - People Watch
Italy or Bust

Lee Martino, recently departed chief operating officer of The Easton Company before its acquisition last month by Denver's Pratt-Miles, was spotted this week in Florence, Italy.

Martino has reportedly enrolled for studio art classes at La Bottega dell'Arcimboldo. Martino's family plans to join him before the holidays once his children's winter break begins. Locals report that Martino is leasing a villa on the outskirts of the city.

Asked in a phone interview with our business editor if he had given up corporate life, Martino replied, "Does anyone really care what I'm doing now?"

Actually Lee, we only care whose money you're doing it with. *Meow.*

What Do You Give as a Farewell Gift to a Guy Worth Ninety Million Dollars? Redux

Two weeks after the sale of The Easton Company closed, the payroll manager and one of the accountants were going thorough a stack of Jeffrey Elkins' final business expenses for reimbursement. Most of the items seemed fairly routine, although they shook their heads and trash talked about the moving company bill for his office furniture.

Near the bottom of the stack was a small yellow handwritten receipt from a boutique jeweler in the city reflecting a purchase on Jeffrey Elkins' platinum company credit card. It read:

10 antique lapel pins $10,000.

Grounded

The week after the merger closed in November, pilot Jake Martin received a call from Jeffrey Elkins. "I'm still in negotiations with George Miles about the transfer of Easton Transportation," Jeffrey told him. "Keep your head low, and I'll get back to you as soon as I know more." Then a handful of weeks passed where Jake received no work calls, emails, or any other contact from the old or new owner. Since Jake had spent much of the past three months on the ground, the hangar was in pristine shape and his flight records and reports were all up to date.

There wasn't much to do each day except chill out at the hangar waiting for a call and swapping stories and speculations with the contract copilot and mechanic who stopped by regularly to see if there was any news. Jake envied them. As contractors they had worked for Easton but not exclusively, which meant they were still actively working and flying regularly. They were starting to kid Jake about cobwebs developing between his limbs and the floor. By Thanksgiving, Jake was itchy enough to find reasons to roll each of the two planes out of the hangar at least once a week and start their engines, just to assure himself everything checked out OK. It was as close as he was getting to flying and provided some reassurance that he was truly still a working pilot.

It was well into December when an internal auditor from Pratt-Miles showed up at the hangar unannounced one weekday morning. Jake had walked out of the office into the hangar bay just in time to see a young man, bulging briefcase in hand, spinning slowly in a circle as he looked up at the two planes. "Oh my. Wow," Jake heard him say.

Putting on his best smile, Jake walked toward the stranger and extended his hand. "Good morning. Welcome. May I help you?" he said, looking the guy directly in the eyes and giving him his best strong military handshake.

Shifting the heavy briefcase to his left hand, the young man shook hands with the pilot and introduced himself. "Oh right. Hello. I'm Mike Taylor from Pratt-Miles in Denver? I'm part of the mid-Atlantic team conducting field audits of properties we've acquired from The Easton Company. Mind if I take a few pictures?"

Easton Transportation – Last Landing

During the subsidiary's existence, detailed information about Easton Transportation's assets and transactions were closely held – corporate lingo for information that's reported but not publicized, and buried among other statistics whenever practical. Not that there were any irregularities to hide from regulators. It just wasn't information company executives wanted wandering through the organization and beyond for exposure to unnecessary scrutiny. Personal use of aircraft by chief executives had been a controversial corporate governance issue for years. SEC and Internal Revenue Service rules concerning the disclosure and definition of personal use versus business use were constantly under review.

Easton Transportation's files had been listed on the voluminous document inventory provided to Pratt-Miles in the weeks before the scheduled merger, but Pratt-Miles had never specifically requested, nor had Easton offered, to send them. It was part of Jeffery Elkins' strategy to buy the subsidiary from the new owner at a reasonable price. The fewer details Pratt-Miles had in advance, the better.

After the close of the sale, the new owner's knowledge about Easton Transportation was little more than a name on a long list of unresolved post-merger items. For several weeks Easton Transportation continued to fly under the radar. Pratt-Miles knew that Easton owned a corporate jet, but that was about the extent of it. The records for Easton Transportation remained in the office of the associate general counsel in Virginia. They were stacked on the floor among other important documents that Pratt-Miles staff in Denver had not yet requested. By year-end, Pratt-Miles executives would finally access those files and learn that Easton Transportation was comprised of the following assets and employees:

- Corporate jet hangar located at Dulles International Airport in Northern Virginia. 10,500 square feet walled off by insulated, interlocking, double-sided steel panels built to withstand the blow of a Mack truck traveling at 50 mph; metal halide lighting and high-gloss Tennant floors emblazoned with the subsidiary's logo – ET – in ten-foot green Edwardian script letters; gated secure complex with twenty-four-hour, Web-accessible security camera mounted in the center of the thirty-three-foot ceiling (this allowed Jeffrey to check on his plane from anywhere in the world by punching it up on his laptop); a plush furnished office and conference room; restrooms with marble countertops, walls and floors; private crew quarters with showers; and a small climate controlled wine cellar.

- Hawker 800A Jet: Serial Number 253718

- Learjet 31A: Serial Number 157824

- Employees: Full-time pilot, co-pilot (contract) and a part-time mechanic (contract)

- All necessary licenses, inspections and contracts for operation of the aircraft and the hangar

- Easton Transportation assessed value: $32.5 million

The discovery came as the new owners began to visit and inventory their recently acquired properties. Ironically, it was Jeffrey Elkins' persistent phone messages to George Miles that expedited the subsidiary's evaluation. Two weeks after the close, Jeffrey Elkins managed to connect with George Miles by phone. Again George did not want to discuss the company jet. "Let me get back to you on that Jeffrey. We just haven't had time to look into it yet, but let me get Legal working on it."

As a *former* CEO, Elkins was gaining awareness that his powers were swiftly shrinking with each passing day. Now an outsider looking in, what else could he do but say "Thanks George. I'll look forward to hearing from you soon."

After another ten days passed without a word from George Miles, Jeffrey placed one more call to the Pratt-Miles CEO. This time George's executive assistant intercepted his call. After briefly discussing the purpose of his call, she gave him George's voice mail, where he left a message asking for a status on Easton Transportation. In his message Jeffrey once again emphasized that he was anxious to move forward with acquiring the subsidiary. Inexperienced with voice mail, Jeffrey caught himself rambling a bit as he left his message. He was accustomed to having his calls taken directly and returned promptly. Leaving recorded messages in the ether was new territory for the former CEO.

A week later Jeffrey received a phone message from George suggesting that Jeffrey should have his attorney get in touch with the Pratt-Miles attorneys "to see what we can work out."

It was around this time – more than a month after the Easton sale had closed – that Dan Strauss stepped into Howard Beck's office at Pratt-Miles headquarters. Howard was Pratt-Miles' chief financial officer and Dan was one of the Pratt-Miles attorneys working on post-merger clean up. After asking for a moment of the CFO's time, Dan placed a folder on Howard's desk and said, "I think you should see this."

"Whatcha got now Dan?" Howard smiled raising an eyebrow.

The past several weeks had been interesting. Usually Howard found himself dealing with fairly mundane stuff in the post-acquisition phase of a merger, but not this time. Long after the close date, they were still uncovering interesting goodies in the pile of Easton merger surprises. Thirteen billion dollars was a big number, but with this merger Pratt-Miles had finally moved up in the world and their well-to-do acquisition had left much undisclosed as all parties rushed to final signature on the deal.

"It's this Easton Transportation thing. You remember George has been getting calls from Jeffrey Elkins about it?"

"Right. I remember. Jeffrey wanted to buy the subsidiary outright before close and we put him off. So what's the status?" Howard asked.

"It seems there's more to this than we realized. One of our site auditors stopped by the Easton headquarters building for the transportation subsidiary documents and files before going out to see the plane. Turns out there are two jets. And that's not all. Well, see for yourself." He flipped open the folder on Howard's desk. Howard quickly scanned the contents. Dan explained this was only a portion of the information the site auditor had emailed that morning. Dan had printed some of the attachments for Howard to see. They included photos of the hangar, the planes, and the financial summary of Easton Transportation's assets.

"Holy crap!" Howard puffed as he looked at the asset page. "Somehow I had the impression from Elkins that this was a modest $5 million subsidiary that had one little ol' plane. No wonder he's been so anxious to take it off our hands."

"So what do we do now?" Dan asked.

"I'll talk to George. I'm going to suggest he stop returning Jeffrey's calls. I'll get in touch with Jeffrey myself about this when the time is right," Howard said.

"So do you think we'll sell these planes or what?" Dan asked.

"Most definitely. But not necessarily to Elkins," the CFO said with a devilish grin. "Do we know which one Jeffrey considered the CEO jet?"

"The Hawker. It was the Hawker he was trying to secure for himself. Apparently, if you read the details, he had it customized to his specifications," Dan explained.

"Okay, thanks Dan. I want to see the rest of the documents when the site auditor gets back."

"No problem," replied Dan, "but what are you up to?" He couldn't help but ask given the tiny smirk on Howard's face. It was clear he was plotting something.

"I'm not quite sure yet. I need to talk to George first. But I promise, I'll let you know how this progresses."

Jeffrey Elkins continued to phone George Miles more and more frequently over the next two weeks, requesting a progress report on his interest in purchasing Easton Transportation. But George never called him back. In a fit of frustration he left a final voice mail for George, "Damn it, George! What the hell's the problem? Enough is enough. It's time to stop this amateur hour behavior and get on with selling me the plane." Then he slammed down the phone.

The next day Jeffrey returned from his morning workout to see the message light blinking on his home office phone. Touching the Play Messages button, he heard the voice of Howard Beck, Pratt-Miles' CFO. "Good morning, Jeffrey. Hope you're doing well. Just getting back to you about your request to buy the Hawker. If you want your plane so badly, feel free to bid on it. You'll find it on eBay. Good luck."

Jeffrey's face turned purple with rage. "That bastard," he seethed. "He can't be serious."

Jeffrey had never visited the eBay website but he quickly located it after sitting down at his computer. With all he had heard about the junk people sold on eBay, he never imagined that anyone put jets up for bid. His initial search turned up toy airplanes and model jets, but not multimillion-dollar aircraft. Certainly this was some kind of sick joke Beck was playing on him. Then it occurred to him to enter "aircraft" in the search box. And there it was – his customized Hawker 800A listed on eBay. Jeffrey Elkins sat stunned, staring at his computer screen. He couldn't believe this was happening. Nine days, eighteen hours and twenty-seven minutes later, Jeffrey Elkins' customized Hawker sold on eBay for $6,235,100.

The Hero's Farewell

The day after the Hawker sold on eBay, Jeffrey received an overnight Fed Ex package from the Pratt-Miles Denver headquarters. There was no note inside the envelope – only a paperback. It was a book that Jeffrey was not familiar with. The title was The Hero's Farewell: What Happens When CEOs Retire, written by Jeffrey Sonnenfeld and published by the Oxford University Press. The back cover noted that Business Week had named it one of "The Ten Best Business Books of the Year." A small orange plastic self-adhesive tab extended from a page near the front of the book, inviting Jeffrey to flip to it. Two paragraphs on the right hand page were highlighted in bright orange:

> Among retiring leaders, chief executives experience the greatest tensions and must face an especially challenging retirement transition, for over their careers their purpose and self-worth have become increasingly linked to the well being of the firm. The chief executive becomes the personal symbol of the institution. Within his or her own organization, the chief executive becomes a folk hero.

> A retired CEO faces difficult challenges in seeking meaningful self-purpose. Stepping into alternative jobs and roles of lower stature can be difficult and rare. The challenge is how to find meaningful post-CEO employment for a retired executive whose work skills are not so easily utilized or transferable. For example, violinists in retirement can still offer solo performances or play with small ensembles. A conductor, however, needs the full orchestra to be employed, and thus a conductor's skills are not usually portable into retirement.

"Folk hero my ass," Jeffrey muttered. Reaching the end of the passage, Jeffrey angrily tossed the book across the room toward his desk. Between leaving his hand and landing on the desktop, a piece of paper fell out of the book and onto the floor. Jeffrey picked it up and turned it over. It was a glossy photo of the Hawker.

The Stuff at Iron Mountain

The business records environment is exploding with billions of paper documents, trillions of electronic messages, and exabytes of electronic records – all of which must be managed.

– Iron Mountain corporate website

There was a time in American corporations when "business file management and retention" referred to sliding walls of rotating steel cabinetry containing thousands of manila folders sporting colored labels. These files were organized by indexes cataloged in a library of notebooks. A full-time employee was often hired to be the strict guardian of the files.

That was before the advent of desktop computers and the information age. Once an office was no longer dependent on fast typists, carbon paper, and white correction fluid to produce quality correspondence, documents and reports, the amount of paper generated within organizations quickly quadrupled. The paper explosion was initially fueled by Xerox copiers and later expanded when teams of word processing employees replaced typing pools. Suddenly offices, desks and files were awash in dot matrix printouts, and soon, laser printer reports. Although some organizations had begun copying records to microfiche as early as the 1950s, it was a time-consuming process requiring cameras, a pricey fiche reader, and excellent eyesight.

Most of this evolution took place in the 1980s before the widespread use of floppy disks, email, CDs and PDAs. The result was a paper usage explosion. Instead of circulating one copy of a memo or a report to several employees who each read it, initialed it, and passed it along to the next recipient, everyone got their own copy of every document. This resulted in multiple people throughout an organization sending the same documents to be filed and stored. Consequently, most offices in the early days of word processing and desktop computing devoted as much floor space to file storage as to desks and chairs.

During this paper era some managers preached shredding and disposal as the solution to exponential paper accumulation. Viewed as "old school" to suggest destruction of unnecessary documents and records, these managers were actually ahead of their time. They understood that it was folly for companies to accumulate such an extensive paper trail and commit so much business practice to writing.

One notable Easton human resources director admonished his staff in the mid-1980s, "If you don't have to put it in writing, then don't. If I'm ever compelled to take the stand in some court case, I'd like to have an opportunity to explain our actions without some attorney waving a piece of paper in my face." At the time this HR director seemed to be a management dinosaur; history proves he was a corporate visionary.

A few seasons into this new communications era, corporate budget analysts began to recognize the value of sending more files to offsite storage. Office space was too expensive in most geographic locations to keep all that paper amassed in-house. Many larger organizations previously utilized some offsite file storage, but mostly to store decades of historical information or specialty materials. Now suddenly almost every organization and corporation in America needed more offsite storage capacity.

Enter Iron Mountain. In business since 1951, Iron Mountain morphed over the decades, adapting to serve the growing needs of the international business community by providing records management solutions for all media and formats, including paper, digital, film, and tape.

The history of Iron Mountain is worth a peek. How does a company come to provide record storage to ninety-eight percent of the Fortune 1000, and serve over 90,000 organizations in twenty-six countries? Believe it or not it began with mushroom farming.

For more than fifteen years, Herman Knaust, a.k.a. The Mushroom King, grew and marketed mushrooms in the Hudson River Valley in a depleted iron ore mine purchased in 1936 for $9,000. After World War II, Knaust was searching for an alternative use for his mine. Cold War apprehensions and the arrival of the atomic age convinced Knaust there was a market for protecting information from war and lesser disasters. When the first vaults of Iron Mountain Atomic Storage opened, Knaust located a sales office in the Empire State Building and invited national figures such as General Douglas MacArthur to tour the facilities. New York City banks, followed by other high profile establishments, soon began moving vital records to storage in Iron Mountain. Aligning with business demands for more offsite storage, Iron Mountain spread beyond the New York City market in 1980. It bought its first storage warehouse in Boston in 1983 and expanded into management and retention of legal and medical documents. Then in 1988, Iron Mountain acquired Bell and Howell Records Management, Inc., a company four times its size, and became the first national service provider in the industry. In little more than a decade, Iron Mountain grew from $100 million to $2.7 billion in annual revenues.

Herman Knaust wasn't joking in 1952 when he told the *Wall Street Journal,* "This business will mushroom." Clearly organizations worldwide have been quite busy since the launch of the information age storing masses of documentation. The Easton Company was not unique in contributing to the stockpiles.

After a merger, what happens to all those archived files and other important and not so important documents that a corporation sends to offsite storage? Acquiring companies such as Pratt-Miles groan at the task of reviewing stored company records when they buy a well-established corporation like The Easton Company.

During a merger, stored records is an area that seldom receives the attention it deserves, unless someone is looking for a particular missing legal document that is integral to the sale. The Easton Company's records represented decades of boxed and indexed documents and bits of corporate history that, at some point in time, someone believed were worth saving.

In the transition period when Pratt-Miles continued to uncover information about Easton, Pratt-Miles presented extensive lists requesting specific key documents from the Easton legal division. As the selling company, Easton produced the requested records either from onsite files throughout the company or from storage. In the course of Pratt-Miles' acquisition of Easton, that's where the document review process stopped – at least until after the sale closed.

Occasionally, an acquiring company might go one step further by asking to review a master list of files in storage. Generally the file review focuses on accounting, human resources, legal and tax matters. The master lists usually provide only vague hints as to what might be found in a particular stored box. Indexed box descriptions normally list the month and year the box was stored, the division or department sending it, and the last name of the lowly clerk who sent the box to storage. The contents description field on the form might be left blank or contain one word (PENSIONS) or a short phrase (BENEFIT BOOKLETS) to guide future employees on a hunt for some long forgotten but suddenly necessary bit of arcane information.

The other key bit of information that must be completed on the form before a box can go to offsite storage is the storage time period. Here, the employee sending the box to storage checks: one year, five years, ten years, or indefinitely. Finally, the storage form requires the sender to indicate instructions for the storage company to follow when the storage time period has elapsed. The choices are: "contact sender for new storage instructions" or "destroy."

Few corporate clerks and administrators are ever trained in the process of sending files to offsite storage. Insufficiently informed and not wanting to throw caution to the wind, clerks packing boxes for storage frequently check the "indefinitely" box. Without any other direction, this seems like the safe choice. The lack of training and guidance regarding this one small procedural detail probably accounts for a significant portion of Iron Mountain's ongoing business.

A more inquisitive acquiring company might perform core sampling once the master list of documents is reviewed – for example, sending for every seventh box in storage from the past seven years, plus any others with intriguing contents descriptions (PARTY DOLLS).

Inevitably, when an acquiring company digs through stored corporate files, the new management's reaction is universally predictable: Why the heck were they saving this stuff?

In the throes of an acquisition, however, sifting through stored documents was a low priority for Pratt-Miles. In the short window between the announcement of the sale and the close of the deal, they barely had time to review the piles of pertinent documents required to effect the merger. After the acquisition, Easton corporate records remained at Iron Mountain with periodic review ticklers and invoices redirected to the new owner.

Although no one wanted to give it much thought, eventually low level Pratt-Miles administrative staff had to consider what might be in storage. After several months of notices and invoices from Iron Mountain, a part-time Pratt-Miles accounting clerk asked the question, "Do you think we need to continue storing all these Easton files at Iron Mountain?"

"Oh heavens. Please don't ask," a coworker responded. "They might make us actually go through it all."

Eventually, after a merger deal closes, someone must make a decision about the future of the former corporation's stored documents. Either keep them, or shred and destroy. But is it an all-or-nothing decision, or will some detective work occur beforehand?

What makes management uncomfortable is the material that corporate attorneys automatically assume is out there: documents related to a lawsuit-in-waiting. Such records are like Rip Van Winkle asleep under the tree; only this stuff sleeps underground in an old mining mountain in the northeastern rural countryside.

Fifteen months after the acquisition, Pratt-Miles decided to stop opening all mail addressed to The Easton Company or any former Easton employees. It was shredded upon delivery. A few weeks later, a decision was made about Easton files stored at Iron Mountain. Pratt-Miles would undertake one final review of the material, decide what to keep and what to toss, and (more importantly) document the prudence of the review process.

One Pratt-Miles attorney shared her thoughts about the matter off-the-record with a coworker, "It would be nice to send word to the mysterious recordkeeping elves that everyone imagines work at Iron Mountain and tell them to destroy it all, but we just can't do that without having some basis for our decision." It was the in-house attorneys who insisted on sending for a vanload of assorted boxes to have staff take a cursory look and hopefully confirm it was all worthless and disposable.

Sending for the Iron Mountain boxes was like taking a geologic core sample. There were decades of history here: some of it interesting, some of it amusing, most of it irrelevant. But like a core sample, it had to be studied carefully to know what critical items might be lurking below the surface.

A Pratt-Miles administrative assistant paused in the middle of flipping through stacks of Easton printed material. She glanced at the other workers around the table who were buried in old Easton files. They had sorted out a tiny "keep" pile while their "shred" pile was now bigger than a compact car.

"This is the nonsensical paper garbage that some future intergalactic dynasty will unearth and sift through to discover the secrets of the post-atomic era," one employee said. "Sadly, what they will discover will be the least interesting, most useless information imaginable – in triplicate." Included in the last shipment of boxes from Iron Mountain was one inventoried as "HRH docs/gloves/goggles." This description had caught the attention of a Pratt-Miles law clerk taking a concluding look at the storage inventory lists. It was sufficiently captivating to request that bin in the final run.

Are You Still a Corporate Pilot If There Are No Corporate Planes?

Jake Martin stood in the doorway of the hangar bay as the new owner of the Hawker 800A taxied toward the runway. It hurt too much to watch it take off with someone else in his seat, so he turned and walked back into the empty bay. The pilot for the new corporate owner of the Learjet had flown it away two days before. Without the planes, the Easton Transportation hangar was depressingly lonely.

Jeffrey had sent Jake a note right after the planes had sold, saying he was angry with Pratt-Miles for their poor handling of the situation and sorry to see the Hawker go. "It's like losing a good friend," Jeffrey had written.

"You're telling me," Jake had mumbled to himself as he read Jeffrey's note.

The note continued, "My apologies that things didn't work out as I'd expected. No doubt you will land on you feet – snatched up by another CEO who appreciates the comfort of being flown by the very best. Best of luck, Jeffrey Elkins."

Jake strolled through the hangar to the office and took a small set of keys from his top desk drawer. Then he walked into the conference room and unlocked the wine cabinet. He extracted a bottle of 2003 Screaming Eagle Cabernet and opened it. It was expensive – one of Jeffrey's favorites – and certainly one Jake might enjoy when someone else was paying. As he walked back through the hangar he stopped dead center and took his first swig. It was smooth and fine. Jake chuckled quietly to himself. Good? Yes. Excellent? Definitely. But only the corporate elite on an expense account would spend $500 for 25.6 ounces of fermented grape juice.

Looking up at the camera installed in the ceiling, Jake smiled and raised the bottle in his hand. "Hey Jeffrey. How's it going? If you're watching, this moment is depressing as hell." After taking another swig, "Lucky you. You're not here."

After the holidays at the start of the New Year, Jake was continually amazed every other Friday when he checked his bank account balance and confirmed he was still receiving his direct deposited paychecks from Pratt-Miles. The contract copilot and mechanic had received their letters terminating their work agreements weeks ago.

Toward the end of January, Jake got a call from a human resources manager at Pratt-Miles in Denver. After exchanging some surreal pleasantries with a person he had never met, the manager asked Jake if he would mind staying on for a couple more months to handle the run-out of bills and expenses related to the close of Easton Transportation. Jake agreed, thinking to himself this would be easy to handle while he geared up to look for new employment.

The following week, another call came from Denver. This time it was from a member of the corporate legal group. "I realize this isn't what you normally *do*," the young-voiced female attorney purred into the phone with the emphasis on the word do, "but we were wondering if you would mind acting as the company's agent over the next couple months. We really need someone to show the hangar to potential buyers and, well…you would be the perfect person to do that, don't you think?"

Jake was quiet, not to be rude, but truly thinking over the ramifications of what the woman was asking.

"We don't mean to insult you – really," the attorney jumped into the silence. "We know that as a professional pilot you might be insulted that we're asking, but here's the deal. We'd be happy to continue your current salary for the next few months if you'd agree to show the hangar as needed. We'd send you a Blackberry so that you could come and go as you please, as long as you would make yourself reasonably available to meet an interested buyer at their convenience. But again, we would understand if you said no. As a fellow trained professional I can appreciate that you are probably anxious to get back to what you love to do most."

"Let me think on this overnight, if that's alright with you," Jake responded. "I'll call you back in the morning with my answer."

"Fine. Really. That would be great. We'll wait to hear from you."

Jake flipped his cell phone shut and began considering the proposal Pratt-Miles was making. The attorney was right. It was an insult to ask a pilot of his caliber to work as the Vanna White of the Hangar, so to speak. But on the other hand, they were willing to pay generously for him to unlock the facility and conduct show and tell tours with wealthy investors.

Two weeks later, a Blackberry toting Jake Martin was sitting just outside the Easton Transportation hangar doors, enjoying one of those freak unseasonably warm winter days that pop up almost annually in the Washington area. Tipped back in a folding chair leaning against the outer wall of the hangar, Jake was killing time watching planes land. Jake wore his tour guide garb: black leather flight jacket, pilot cap, and his best and newest aviator sunglasses, which glinted in the sunshine and gave his wide white smile an air of mystery. He was waiting for yet another potential buyer scheduled to tour the hangar. Someone named Carolee Kelly. With a name like that he was certain she would look like all the other female millionaires who had already visited, consistently arriving in enormous limos: tall, anorexic bleached-out women with impossibly high heels and ridiculously small dogs residing full-time in designer bags. The dogs usually wore couture clothes that sometimes matched their owners' outfits. There had been plenty of interested businessmen who passed through dressed in Briani, Armani or Hugo Boss suits, mirror shades that rivaled his own, and Rolexes the size of mantel clocks. The phrase "ludicrous outrageous wealth" continuously snaked though Jake's consciousness every time he gave another tour.

On this beautiful winter day, Jake felt like he had sold his soul. He desperately missed flying, but the money Pratt-Miles was paying him while he freely roamed with a Blackberry on his hip made his decision to defer job hunting an easy one. Almost daily he went through the mental gymnastics of reminding himself that he was a professional pilot – it was important to remember that. However, this period was the first time in his entire life when he was able to relax on the job. "Just a little while longer," he told himself each new day. "Just a few more weeks."

Tales of the Sofa

Three weeks after the close, with more than 110 corporate jobs already eliminated, nearly half the offices in the former headquarters building stood unoccupied. Entire sections of the building, including two back entrance hallways, were left dark when employees arrived in the morning. Employees entering through any of the doors other than the main entrance now had the strange sensation of entering a deserted building. It was eerie. Just a month before – and every business day for decades before that – the building had possessed its own soundtrack of voices, phones, footfalls on hardwood floors, and the general buzz and hum of generations of office equipment. Now it was like entering a morgue. Dark and quiet. Too quiet for a building this size. The phones had stopped ringing. The sound of conversations, meetings, laughter and even the hum of the lights and electronics was disturbingly subdued or absent.

Occasionally, an employee from one floor of the building would wander to another floor to find a fellow human to talk to for a few minutes. The conversation usually began with, "Got a minute? Everyone left in my group is traveling this week except me. It's a little lonely up there."

In those early days of December when the daylight hours were seasonally scarce, the dark and quiet atmosphere inside the former headquarters was more than some remaining employees could tolerate. During those closing weeks of the year, it was commonplace for a worker to stand up and announce in a relatively loud voice some version of: "It's too quiet in this place. I gotta get out of here for a while." And out the person would go for fresh air and the comfort of some coffee shop noise. On cloudy days someone usually walked around and turned on lights in portions of the unoccupied spaces saying, "I know it's wasteful but I just can't stand it being so dark in here. It's depressing enough – we don't need to make it gloomier."

On one of those gloomy days, a marketing specialist walked through the main level intent on shedding a little more light throughout the building. On a whim, she flipped on the lights in the CEO's reception suite. Later that morning, because it was an exceptionally gray and quiet day, Kate Cooper and two remaining human resources employees decided to take their meeting to a new location in the building, hoping for some better light and some new perspective. Turning a corner on the main level, Kate noticed the lights on in the CEO's suite.

"Wow, that's eerie," Kate's said, stopping at the executive suite entrance. Set apart from other offices on the floor, the suite was out of the way and easy to ignore, especially once the furnishings were removed and the space was left dark. But with the lights on, it caught her interest and attention. "You don't think..." she began, then stopped, turning to look at her workmates.

Jim Fisher chuckled and immediately strode confidently into the entryway of the suite, calling over his shoulder, "Oh you've got to be kidding me, Kate. You don't really think the $90 million man has gotten homesick and felt the need to return to his former office for one last pensive visit, do you?" Kate chuckled, and along with Sylvia Carter followed Jim into the empty reception area of the suite. "I'm not sure I've ever been in here before, have you?" Jim turned and asked

"Oh yes," Kate replied. "Several times. All memorable but none of them particularly enjoyable. Even the social visit when I was invited to come meet Jeffrey for the first time was awkward and sweaty."

"Sweaty?" Jim turned to Kate with a huge grin on his face. "You don't really mean *sweaty*, do you?"

"Not that kind of sweaty, you moron. I was referring to the first time I entered Jeffrey Elkins' office and was formally introduced to him. When he shook my hand it was sweaty – his hand, I mean. His hand!" Kate's lame explanation had accelerated Jim's chuckles into a belly laugh.

"Kate, my dear, that wasn't sweat," Jim managed, gasping for air between fits of expelled laughter. "That was the antibacterial gel he squirted into his hands just before you walked in." At that line, all three of them dissolved in a good laugh – something they hadn't shared for quite a while.

The door leading into Jeffrey's office was ajar, but the space beyond was dark. "Come on, let's go," Sylvia said after they recovered from the joke.

"What's wrong? You're not scared are you?" Jim smiled as he looked at Sylvia.

"Not scared, Fisher, just a little spooked. It's sort of creepy in here with the furniture all gone and the blinds drawn. Let's get out of here and find someplace comfy to meet."

"Not until I get a peek into what was once the cerebral engine room of this place." Jim moved toward the office door.

"Wait a sec, Jim," Kate said. "I don't know why but somehow this feels like we're doing something wrong. I know that's crazy, but I'm with Sylvia. Let's save this adventure for another day."

"Hey, no one said you had to join me. But I am definitely not leaving without a tour of the executive washroom. I may not get a second chance. They could deliver my walking papers any day now," Jim continued, only half jokingly.

"Okay, okay, we'll go with you, but we're not staying," Kate said in her best motherly tone.

"What's wrong, Kate? Worried someone will catch us in here?"

"I suppose something like that," she replied. Sylvia was looking more worried as she gripped her legal notepad close to her chest.

Pulling the door open wide and stepping confidently into what had been Jeffrey Elkins' office, Jim raised his voice, "Don't be such wusses, ladies. There's nothing left here to fear," and then Jim's voice dissolved into another round of uncontrollable laughter.

"What the heck's so darn funny?" Sylvia insisted, losing some of her hesitancy and taking a few steps toward the door.

"Just come see. There're really no words to describe it." That statement changed the two women's caution to curiosity and they walked quickly into the dark office. "Take a look at that," Jim pointed to a far corner of the otherwise empty room. "Can you believe it?" The three again lost their composure in a new round of giggles and snorts.

"I claim it," Jim said when he finally managed to stop laughing. "It's mine 'til I'm gone."

"Tell me you're not serious," Kate responded. "Where will you put it?"

"In my office."

"You can't do that," the two women replied simultaneously.

"Who's going to stop me? The merger police?"

"Seriously, Jim," Kate began.

"Don't use that mother superior tone with me, Kate. With the run up to the holidays, we're not expecting a visit from anyone in the Denver office until year-end when they show up with the next round of pink slips. You and I both know my name is probably on that list. So in the meantime I might as well work in luxury. Unless you want it, of course. Since you still outrank me post-merger I would defer to you if you want it," Jim gave Kate a courtly bow.

"No I don't want it," Kate said taking a step back.

"There's no room for that in your office, Fisher," Sylvia noted, returning to practical matters.

"And how would you move it?" Kate joined in. "It's got to weigh a ton."

"I'll find a way," Jim said.

"You're crazy, Jim. That thing won't even fit thorough your office door."

"Then I'll just have to change offices again. There are plenty to choose from. There's got to be one somewhere in our area that will accommodate this fine specimen."

Just then a female voice called from out in the hallway, "Yoo hoo – anybody in there?" Kate recognized the voice. It was Jane Richards, one of the administrative assistants who no longer had a manager. Without anyone to provide her with work to do Jane spent a good part of every day wandering the building and getting into everyone else's business.

"We're in here Jane," Kate called back. "Just doing a little HR tour of the offices. No reason for concern." An important statement to make since Jane, without any other mission, was suspected of being the latest snitch, providing details of activities great and small back to Pratt-Miles management in Denver. "Come on, Jim. Let's exit gracefully," Kate whispered. "I'm not interested in providing Jane any new gossip."

"I'm not leaving until I pee in the executive toilet," Jim hissed back. At that Sylvia's face turned pale and she started to back toward the door. Before Kate could respond, Jane appeared in the doorway.

"Well, look who it is," she said in her affected lilt. "What brings you all in here?" Jane chattered, walking toward Jim, Kate and Sylvia. Then she pulled up short and both hands shot up to cover her mouth, which had suddenly dropped open as she pronounced, "Oh-my-word!" Jim stepped aside so Jane could get a better look at the focus of their attention.

"Like it?" Jim smiled at Jane. "It's my new sofa. I'm already taking names to see who gets it when I'm gone. We'll have a drawing or a raffle or something. It'll be great. I might even make it a fundraiser. What do you think, Jane? Wanna get in on this?" The look on Jane's face was too much for Kate to bear. She erupted in laughter, and was joined by Sylvia and Jim.

"You can't be serous," Jane gawked.

"Oh but I am. This is one serious piece of history. I think it needs a better home."

"But it doesn't belong to you," Jane pointed out.

"I didn't say it did. I just plan to use it just like my other office furniture until I leave."

Jane looked surprised, "You know you're leaving?"

"Jane. Get a grip. Most of us are leaving. That's how this merger thing works. Now run along and make your call to Denver. Be sure to tell them it's the yellow sofa from Jeffrey's office with the Easton logo. Don't leave out any details. And don't incriminate Sylvia and Kate – they're just innocent observers." Jim stopped talking and folded his arms across his chest, giving Jane one of his best big fake smiles.

"Well, I…." Jane sputtered. Clearly Jim had left her at a loss for words. She blinked twice then backed out the door.

As they heard her walking swiftly away Jim called, "Bye Jane. Give the folks in Denver my love."

The next morning, the yellow sofa had replaced the small round worktable and chairs in Jim's office. It now sat directly under Jim's favorite new piece of office art: a three-by-five-foot framed poster of a horse clearly captioned "COW." Jim had hung it on his wall the week after the merger closed. Whenever anyone asked him what it meant, he replied, "It's a reminder. In the world of mergers and acquisitions, you can label it anything you want. Regardless of what someone chooses to call it – the thing is what it is. Don't be fooled."

Admiring the sofa, Jim was already gleefully anticipating the arrival of the Pratt-Miles human resources team from Denver later in the month. Janice Foss, the vice president, was a petite fifty-something platinum blonde with skinny legs who sported stiletto heels, short skirts, trendy jackets and chunky jewelry. Janice had made a lasting impression on former Easton employees the day the sale closed. Speaking to a group of employees who had not lost their jobs that day, she had responded to one employee's "What's going to happen to us next?" question with a terse, "Get over it. Enough of this Easton angst. Just get over it and move on." That little speech was delivered an hour after the first forty Easton employees had been pink-slipped and told to clean out their desks and exit the building. Janice Foss had not made any friends that day in their offices – or since.

It didn't take much effort for Jim to imagine Janice walking into his office and deliberately closing the door, her nail extensions clicking against the knob. Clutched in her other hand would be a manila envelope containing his termination paperwork. He knew exactly how the meeting would go. As a human resources rep, he had witnessed plenty of these meetings over the past few weeks. Though if all went according to plan, Janice's meeting with Jim would be just a little different.

Janice was big on making a deliberate entrance and swift exit for these reduction-in-force tête-à-têtes. It was part of her routine. Jim was looking forward to inviting her to take a seat on the sofa – the only place to sit in his office – to deliver her little talk. When she was done with her "thanks for everything, we won't be needing your services any longer" speech, he planned to be intently studying his paperwork as she attempted to stand up. It gave him great pleasure knowing that she would require his gentlemanly assistance to get out of the sofa and depart. He planned to make her ask for help. After all, she would have just told him she no longer needed his services.

A Merry Christmas…

When George Miles and the members of his executive team traveled to the former Easton headquarters for a black tie holiday party, it was only their second visit since the merger. That evening the celebration took full advantage of the many unique spaces in the former Easton headquarters building by selecting different venues for food tables, bars and entertainment throughout the two upper floors. George and his CFO, Howard Beck, strolled with their wives into the former boardroom. A chef was serving lobster delicacies and bits of prime rib on focaccia, but the small group was drawn to the windows and the reflection of the moon in the surface of the lake outside.

"Wow, that's quite amazing," George said, using the blood orange martini in his hand to point toward the view.

"Not half as amazing as this," replied his wife, who was now facing the adjoining wall and staring at a large painting.

"Looks like your typical big corporate art to me," Howard noted, after a quick glance at the large unframed canvas.

"Then you'd better look again. In fact," she continued, stepping up to the piece and staring more closely at the signature in the lower corner, "you might want to think about getting an art appraiser out here sometime soon. If I'm not mistaken this is an original Jasper Johns from the '60s or early '70s."

"Who's Jasper Johns?" the CFO asked.

"George, darling," Mrs. Miles smiled at her husband, "you really need to send your numbers guy here for a little art education."

Howard's wife cringed and gave her husband the "shut up and don't say another word" look.

"Is it valuable?" Howard Beck's voice broke slightly as he glanced from one female face to the other.

207

Andrea Miles gave Howard Beck's wife a sympathetic grin and said, "I'll send over my art history books when we get back to Denver."

"Wait a minute," Beth Beck said turning back at the CEO's wife. "Does that mean those paintings we passed in the atrium that looked like pop art knock-offs might be the real thing?"

George Miles turned to his wife, the art history major, for some assistance. He knew who Jasper Johns was but he hadn't noticed the paintings in the atrium. He had been busy greeting employees and admiring Sinclair's architectural genius in his design of the building – a true 1960s gem that he and his company now owned.

"I guess we'll find out soon enough," George responded.

"Well, George, lucky you," Andrea Miles cooed. "A 1960s building by one of the world's most famous architects, full of 1960s art by the likes of Peter Max, Jasper Johns and LeRoy Neiman. Let's keep walking, we might find a Warhol in the executive powder room. Looks like it's going to be an especially happy new year."

As the group strolled back through the atrium, George Miles got a silly grin on his face that only his wife observed. Falling back a few paces from the Becks, she took his arm.

"What's so funny Mr. Miles," she enquired tilting her head in a way that made her eyes sparkle in the low party lighting.

"Oh nothing really," George grinned even wider as Andrea squeezed his arm insistently for an honest answer. "It's just that mergers are always such fun, finding out what goodies are in the bottom of the assets box."

"You are a corporate geek," Andrea whispered in his ear, making George blush and smile at the same time. "So what will you do with them if they're originals?" she asked gently.

"Quietly auction them, of course. Why?"

"Oh," Andrea responded flatly.

"But you can have your choice after the official appraisal report is done."

"Oh George," Andrea stopped and leaned over to kiss her husband on the cheek. "You're too good to me."

"Merry Christmas, darling."

"Merry Christmas, George."

...and a Happy New Year

The measure of a great company will be the way it builds great communities – not how much it saved by screwing its pensioners.

– Joe Trippi
The Revolution Will Not Be Televised

In early December each year, a tidal wave of holiday cards began flooding Easton headquarters. The month after the merger was no different. Fast forward ahead one year, however, and the flood would be barely a trickle, demonstrating just how fickle business relationships really are when a corporate headquarters is transformed into a minor regional office.

For Kate Cooper in human resources, most of the cards came from vendors, consultants, industry peers, law firms, and accounting firms. Then there were always a handful of cards from the company's retirees. You could easily pick them out from the rest. These cards looked nothing like the exquisite art-house, silver-edged, glossy photo greeting cards sent from corporations. By comparison the retiree cards were usually small and the paper cheap; but you could count on the enclosed handwritten notes to be sincerely rich in their sentiments and good wishes. They were from real people, not from corporations.

Among the holiday greetings from retirees that December – less than a month after the Pratt-Miles purchase of The Easton Company – was a dime store card printed in China with the following note written in shaky cursive blue ink:

The best Christmas gift I am given each year is my Company medical insurance. If there is ever anything I can do for the great people at The Easton Company – please let me know.

Kate fought back tears as she read those words, written by an 84-year-old former payroll clerk, knowing this would likely be the last year retirees would be receiving this "gift."

In the News

May 8
Pratt-Miles Cuts Easton Retirees' Health Benefits

WASHINGTON (Corporate Wire) – Pratt-Miles Inc. (PMI), which bought The Easton Company last year, is eliminating retiree benefits for hundreds of former Easton employees. Pratt-Miles has sent letters to approximately 400 retirees and their surviving spouses advising them that their medical and life insurance benefits will end later this year. Pratt-Miles officials said the move was made to bring the benefits of the Easton retirees in line with those of Pratt-Miles retirees.

As it turned out, Jeffrey Elkins never made a recommendation to continue benefits for Easton retirees. He never talked to George Miles about a generation of employees who had stuck with The Easton Company to earn post-retirement health care benefits. In fact, no discussion ever occurred between Jeffrey Elkins and George Miles about Easton's retirees or the company's retiree benefits. Retiree advocacy was never on Jeffrey's short list of issues once Pratt-Miles made their purchase offer.

When the merger proxy statement was released in late September, long-service Easton employees were displeased about its lack of information concerning the future of the retiree benefits package. At an employee meeting hosted by the Pratt-Miles transition team at Easton's headquarters in October, the Q&A session quickly turned to that topic.

Active employees who had already worked enough years to be eligible for retirement wanted answers. They asked the Pratt-Miles human resources representative at the meeting if they should retire before the deal closed. The response was not reassuring. The Pratt-Miles meeting moderator actually read a prepared response from a piece of paper: "The new owner will provide benefits substantially similar, in aggregate, to benefits provided to similarly situated employees of Pratt-Miles."

"That doesn't really answer the question," a male voice from the audience chided. "Is it in our best interest to retire before the merger closes, or wait until after?"

"That's a personal decision. It's entirely up to you. Remember there are no guarantees either way," the HR representative stated.

"Exactly what is that supposed to mean?" another employee shot back.

"Well, you can retire now and become an Easton retiree with benefits. But there's no guarantee those benefits will continue indefinitely once Pratt-Miles owns Easton. If you need health insurance, you might be better off continuing to work."

"So are you saying I will have a job with Pratt-Miles after the close?" another employee asked.

"You know we can't guarantee that. Pratt-Miles is still in the process of evaluating staffing needs," the meeting moderator answered.

"Then what do you suggest we do?" another employee pressed.

"Again, that's entirely up to you," came the reply.

"Thanks for the useful information," an attendee in the front row huffed sarcastically.

"Any time," the moderator from Pratt-Miles cheerily answered, without the least bit of concern in her voice.

Individuals who had already retired from The Easton Company did not learn that Pratt-Miles had no retiree benefit plans until months after they had cast their votes for the merger. Spread across the country, the majority of Easton retirees were aware of the Easton/Pratt-Miles merger, but had no idea their own retiree medical and life insurance benefits were in jeopardy until they received letters on Pratt-Miles stationery six months after the sale closed. The Easton retirees were shocked and irate. They had spent their careers with Easton and had been repeatedly told, both verbally and in writing, that their retiree benefits were "for life."

Pratt-Miles gave Easton's retirees six months advance notice before ending benefits. The decision affected nearly 400 retirees and surviving spouses whose ages ranged from fifty-six to ninety-four.

The retirees asked, "What about all those benefits memos, retirement letters and booklets The Easton Company distributed promising retiree medical benefits for life?" Pratt-Miles simply declared them invalid, unless they were specifically incorporated into a written severance agreement that was witnessed and signed by both parties. Of course, the only retirees holding that type of a document were Easton's former executives. Certainly not the secretaries and janitors who had spent careers typing and sweeping floors for a secure retirement.

Retirees wrote to their congressional representatives. They spoke with reporters. They consulted attorneys. Legal action was threatened. Possibly a class action lawsuit. Unfortunately, the same law designed to protect workers' benefits – the Employee Retirement Income Security Act, or ERISA – also creates a series of hurdles that an individual must jump before going to court. In a case like this, those ERISA hurdles can take two years or more to complete. Only after exhausting all remedies under ERISA can a person bring suit against an employer in court. It did not require a genius in the Pratt-Miles legal department to realize that time was on the corporation's side in this matter. Chances were good that the company could wait out the aging retirees, who would run out of money or run out of time before the case was resolved.

Peace of Mind? Passé

The envelope arrived in her mail soon after Pratt-Miles advised Easton retirees that their benefits were being terminated. Kate Cooper ripped opened the hand addressed catalog-sized mailer with the assorted postage stamps affixed to it and pulled out a small booklet whose pages were yellowing and curled at the edges. Attached to it was a note from Samuel Jones, an Easton retiree who had joined the company in 1965 and retired thirty-one years later in 1996. His note read:

Kate,

Get a load of this. What's happened to my piece of the "peace of mind" I was promised? You'll notice there's no disclaimer and Ed Easton's printed signature along with his endorsement of the company's terrific retiree benefits program is on the inside cover.

Can someone please explain to me in plain English how Pratt-Miles can legally get away with ending these benefits for all of us with no more effort than if they were turning off a spigot?

An Easton Retiree 'Til the Day I Die,

Samuel Jones

214

The front cover of the booklet included a 1960s-looking cartoon of a happy little man in a suit reaching up to a tree whose leaves spelled out "Enjoyable Retirement." On the first page, Kate found this introduction:

Retirement with Financial Comfort

It helps anyone's peace of mind all through life to know he's going to be sitting safe, financially, in his later years.

That goes for the girls, too.

We have tried to plan retirement income and benefits for you, which, when added to your social security income and perhaps to income from some personal savings of your own, will give you a comfortable living at retirement.

We pay the entire cost of this retirement plan, so all you have to do is stay with us. We want you to do just that (and happily), and this is one reason we have the retirement benefits plan in the first place.

Kate smiled and shook her head, "Those were the days," she muttered to herself. Pre-ERISA days where trust and a handshake were considered a contract. And a new recognition that "the girls" deserved equal benefits. She sighed sadly. She would forward the booklet to the Pratt-Miles attorneys in Denver but she was certain they would be unmoved.

Tales of the Sofa, Too

Jim Fisher accurately predicted the timing of his own involuntary termination from the company. As a human resources representative, it was easier to see the impending end of one's own job after performing exit interviews for so many others.

Soon after lunch on Jim's last day at work, a small group of employees gathered outside his office for a farewell toast and to share slices of a grocery store sheet cake. This was the downsized version of the more lavish parties historically arranged for people departing the company. As the number of employees leaving started to exceed those who still remained at the former Easton headquarters, the catered going away events gave way to smaller and smaller recognitions.

Sipping Asti Spumante from a plastic champagne glass, Jim joked, "Soon these send-offs will be reduced to a shared bottle of Coke and a bag of pretzels."

What made Jim's going away gathering unique, however, was the auction. After the cake was mostly gone and everyone was on his or her second glass of cheap bubbly, Jim auctioned off the yellow sofa. Conditions of transfer were clearly stated: The highest bidder would be the sofa's next caretaker. The recipient would be responsible for moving the thing to its next location. The auction proceeds would go to Habitat for Humanity.

After three rounds of fast-paced bidding by a half dozen individuals – peppered with lots of hoots and side comments from those assembled – the final bidding faced off between two guys from Information Technology who had been competing with each other for years on everything from the Super Bowl pool to the next promotion. When the bidding hit $260, the IT geeks decided to call a truce and share the sofa. Those assembled clapped and cheered. The spirit of Jim's departure event was something right out of the old Easton Company playbook. A bit of personal recognition wrapped in conviviality, community and charity.

216

Several months later when most members of the IT department were laid off, the yellow sofa once again was without a home. In the wake of the extensive downsizing, an effort was made to consolidate the remaining employees in the building.

It was during this physical office reorganization that the in-house maintenance men were asked to move the yellow sofa out of the old IT area to make room for a group of employees from the third floor. Initially, Lenny and Sam, the only remaining staff from the Easton building maintenance team, protested the manager's request to move the heavy piece of furniture.

"Is it really necessary given all the space throughout the entire building?" Sam wanted to know.

The manager, one of the few who had been reassigned from Denver to Pratt-Miles' newest regional office (the former Easton headquarters building) did not appreciate the push back. "Look fellas. You can't tell me you have that much to do that you can't move a sofa. With the rest of your team already RIFed, I'd think you'd act like you still want a job around here. After all, if we need maintenance help, we can always call a contractor. What you guys do isn't rocket science, you know."

"Okay, okay, okay," Sam finally mumbled to the manager. "Where the heck do you want us to put this thing?"

"I couldn't care less," the manager replied, "as long as it's out of here."

Sam and Lenny exchanged looks. "So you don't care where it goes?" Lenny asked the manager, just to be certain there was no misunderstanding.

"That's correct. But I want it gone by morning." He huffed off and slammed his office door in their faces.

"Well Lenny," Sam grinned, "looks like we have a new sofa for the break room."

Throughout the spring, Lenny and Sam enjoyed lounging on the yellow sofa in the basement break room, adjacent to the maintenance office. It was a fine addition to the other amenities they had collected from throughout the building as more and more employees were let go and offices stood abandoned. The break room already had a recliner, a coffee table, nice floor lamps, two computers for surfing the net, a DVD player and a good-sized TV on a rolling cart acquired from the abandoned communications conference room, nice artwork, several large potted plants, and a small refrigerator from a former lunchroom. Since no one ever came down to the maintenance area, Lenny and Sam were free to entertain themselves during work hours, interrupted only occasionally by a call from someone to fix, move, unlock or clean something.

The sofa was great for catching a nap or settling in to watch an afternoon baseball game on TV. Sam had even entertained his latest lady friend in the break room after normal business hours, letting her in through the downstairs entrance next to the loading dock so she wouldn't have to go past the receptionist or the security guard at the front desk.

"It's the perfect make-out couch," Sam told Lenny, referring to the yellow sofa. "Easy to maneuver around but difficult to escape from."

Unfortunately for Sam and Lenny their good life at work did not last long. Pratt-Miles' Denver management finally determined there was no need for the remaining on-staff maintenance employees. Their jobs were eliminated and they left behind most of the goodies in the break room feathered nest. The maintenance managers had been let go months before. The decision to keep two low level employees was simply for convenience, but now it was clear to the company's new management that an outside contractor could handle any maintenance problems. So on the first of June, Sam and Lenny left the building for the last time, ending the yellow sofa's days of sports, movies and evening amour.

Although Sam and Lenny were sad to go, they had won a $150 bet with the former mailroom workers. The wager was made between the last two mailroom employees and the last two maintenance men. They had bet on who among them would be the last to go. The mailroom clerks were sure they would outlast Sam and Lenny; and they might have won the bet had it not been for their prank or serious error (they never admitted which) involving the Denver office. Soon after another "RIF visit" to the former Easton offices by Janice Foss, the Pratt-Miles vice president of human resources, Janice arrived at her Denver office one morning to find it piled high with Fed Ex packages. There were so many boxes and envelopes that she could barely reach her desk, which was also stacked high with Fed Ex bundles. Closer examination of the packages revealed they had all been sent out from the former Easton mailroom over a three-day period. Every package was addressed to Janice. The Fed Ex shipments included several mass mailings to retirees, vendors and former employees – hundreds of pieces of mail and boxes of materials.

The mailroom staff back in Virginia claimed that the Fed Ex label process must have erroneously repeated Janice's address on all the labels instead of picking up the correct addresses. Janice wasn't buying the explanation. She knew the former Easton personnel didn't like her and the feeling was mutual. It angered her that the mailroom employees didn't even bother to apologize, just shrugged it off by saying, "Oops. Well these things happen."

It took two days for staff in Denver to sort out the mess. Within a month after the Fed Ex fiasco, the mailroom jobs in Virginia were eliminated and the mailroom duties were outsourced. So the last two mailroom employees lost their jobs first, which meant Sam and Lenny won the bet.

Before the merger, The Easton Company's seven-person maintenance crew had a number of important responsibilities, not the least of which was preventive maintenance on the building. Since the exterior was painted stucco adorned with exposed teakwood trellises, ongoing maintenance activities included patching, painting, sanding and staining. Likewise, the storm drainage system required special attention, especially during spring rains and summer storms. The flat-roofed building had been constructed without gutters; so leaf debris from surrounding trees wrecked havoc with the built-in drain lines, which required constant monitoring and periodic cleaning.

When Easton's maintenance managers were laid off, the maintenance director, Ken Bradford, called Pratt-Miles headquarters and spoke with a human resources representative handling the maintenance group's terminations. He wanted to know who to send his files to – the ones containing information on the building's HVAC contracts, scheduled maintenance needs, the key codes to control panels, city fire drill schedules, and building security protocols. The HR rep in Denver said he would get back to Ken, but never did. On his final day at work, Ken tried one last time to contact someone at Pratt-Miles headquarters to pass along what he considered important information. This time he called Janice Foss, the vice president of human resources, on her direct line.

After he explained the reason for his call, Janice responded in a tone one might use when talking to an adolescent, "Ken, you don't have to worry about any of that any more. You just need to let it go so you can move on. I think you've become a bit obsessive about your work. Trust me. We'll manage. Just leave your keys. Thanks again for your concern, but we'll take it from here."

When Ken hung up the phone he was steaming mad. Janice Foss' reply was the most patronizing nonsense he had experienced in his career. Yeah, his was a blue-collar job but he considered himself a professional. He had planned to leave lengthy instructions and notes for someone along with his files. Now, given the vice president's reaction to his interest in transitioning information – and her obvious lack of understanding what his job involved – he cavalierly followed her instructions. Leaving the building that day he simply left his keys on his desk, taking with him over twenty years of knowledge about the operations, quirks and contracts concerning an idiosyncratic building designed by a world class architect.

For the next six months building maintenance was ignored except for the occasional plumbing problem or light fixture issue that required immediate attention. Sam and Lenny, during their short remaining tenure, took a minimalist approach to their work. Preventive maintenance was nonexistent. After Sam and Lenny's departure, no one from Pratt-Miles even thought about such things 2,000 miles away in Denver. Until the roof fell in. Literally.

During the hottest July on record in the Washington area, the air conditioning units stopped working in the Pratt-Miles regional Virginia office. No one seemed to have a clue whether there were service or maintenance contracts on the units since no one had bothered to debrief the maintenance team about anything before they left. Urgent calls placed to Ken Bradford's home number went unanswered. So when the air conditioning stopped working, it took two weeks to find a contractor willing to come take a look at it. It seemed everyone was having brownout issues in the heat, and without a contract, new service requests had to wait their turn.

While waiting for the air conditioning to be repaired in a building with windows that did not open, employees threatened to stop coming to work, left early, called in sick and one even quit. But because the company's owners were in Denver, there was no real urgency on their part. Certainly they wanted the system repaired, but to them it was no big deal.

Then, while the air conditioning was still out, a series of torrential summer storms blew through the metro area and heavy downpours resulted in local flooding. On the third straight day of hard rain, a new maintenance problem occurred that made the lack of air conditioning seem minor by comparison. With the departure of the maintenance staff, no one had cleaned the drains on the top of the building in half a year – a critical task on a building with flat roofs and rooftop terraces. The rainwater pooled on the rooftops and began seeping down inside the walls without anyone noticing until enough water accumulated to cause the collapse of large portions of the ceiling on the lower level of the building.

Employees called the new owners in Denver who seemed baffled as to how a building they recently purchased could be falling down. Employees were moved to other floors, but the water damage was extensive. Structural assessments were required. Mold began to grow on the walls and huge fans and dehumidifying units were set up and run 24/7 for weeks on end while repairs were in progress. Employees complained to management, called in sick, and called OSHA.

It took nearly nine weeks and $3 million to return the building to working order. The ordeal gave Kate Cooper a new crop of gray hairs and a recurring nightmare. In Kate's dream the former headquarters building designed by the famous architect David Sinclair was overgrown with vines. In the dream, as Kate looked on in horror, the overgrown white stucco building sank slowly into a pit of brown muck until it entirely disappeared underground – employees and all – with one big sucking sound. The epilogue in Kate's nightmare was always the same. The new owners viewed the building's demise as a development opportunity and immediately built a twenty-two-story condo tower on the site.

In the News

September 17
THE FORBES 400

A LIST OF THE 400 RICHEST AMERICANS SORTED BY RANK...

#321 George Miles
Net Worth: $1.9 billion
Source: Real Estate
Self made
Age: 56
Marital Status: Married, 2 children
Hometown: Denver, CO
Education: Washington University, Bachelor of Arts/Science

Former mortgage broker developed mixed use projects beginning in 1977. Took Pratt-Miles public in 1992. Relocated business to Denver in 2000. Last year paid $13.1 billion for storied Virginia developer Easton Co.

The same year Pratt-Miles decided to end medical benefits for Easton retirees, George Miles and family moved onto the Forbes 400 for the first time at position 321. On the list of the 400 richest Americans, this placed George Miles just behind the Rockefellers, with a net worth of $1.9 billion.

George Miles celebrated his good fortune by building a mansion on Billionaires' Boulevard in Denver. The new home spanned four city blocks. Conservative estimates placed the cost of the property upon completion at nearly $18 million. The new home included a rooftop solarium, a vast wine cellar, eleven bathrooms, an indoor running track, a climate controlled art gallery and a pipe organ.

Pratt-Miles' move to end benefits for Easton retirees was a basic business decision, according to a statement from the company's management. "It would have been unfair to provide any type of post-retirement benefits to the Easton population when we don't provide anything comparable for our own employees. It's really a matter of equity," the Pratt-Miles spokesman concluded.

Unreported in the press was the number of Easton retirees in their sixties, seventies, eighties and nineties who were thrust into poverty that year, unable to afford medical coverage on their own, and decimated by medical bills.

Pot Luck

Eleven months after the merger closed, a large group of former Easton employees and retirees gathered at a town home in the District of Columbia for a potluck supper reunion. Less than a year ago they had all worked together for the same company. Now only five among those present were still employed by Pratt-Miles. Of those five, two would be laid off by the end of the fiscal quarter.

Most everyone in attendance had found a new job or had decided to retire. Some, already unhappy in their new work environment, were again searching for their next job opportunity. All agreed the work life they had enjoyed at Easton was difficult to replicate elsewhere. A few people talked about lower stress in their new jobs but most mused over days gone by. Everyone agreed what they missed most was the caliber of people they worked with at The Easton Company. The number of former employees who showed up for this potluck dinner on a beautiful fall Saturday evidenced the sentiment.

As the wine and beer flowed the reminiscing intensified. Easton was a forty-eight-year-old company with an entire catalog of corporate stories – good, bad, humorous and embarrassing. Kate Cooper found herself thinking someone should write this stuff down. With everyone now scattered, and so many of the founding employees in their eighties, all this great storytelling could soon be lost.

Clinton Hecker was a retired Easton engineer. He was originally hired by Ed Easton and then worked thirty-five years for the company. Surrounded by a group of both retirees and younger ex-Easton employees, Clinton reminisced about the early days when no one at Easton was making much money but everyone loved the work and lived comfortably. No one, not even the CEO, was wealthy.

"Around the holidays, one day you'd come to work and a Christmas tree would be there in the lobby of the headquarters building. Then another day you'd come to work, and envelopes containing our bonus checks would be pinned to the tree. There was no telling when any of this would happen – no particular schedule – it just did. Then Ed would call us all down to the lobby and we'd have a drink, eat some cookies and open our checks. It was the only time in my life I've ever seen a grown man faint dead away. Yep, Ed was that generous when he could be, and he loved giving. But a big check was a whole lot smaller in those days. A few hundred dollars was a big deal."

Another Easton retiree, Fred Burns, talked about the beginnings of the vacation cottage program, a benefit Ed initiated after striking up an elevator conversation with one of the employees.

"Ed asked the young employee where he was taking his family on vacation that summer. The employee confided to Ed that he really didn't have time to go on vacation, much less the money. So Ed started the cottage program. In those good old days, everyone at headquarters got one week at a mid-Atlantic beach cottage. It didn't matter if you were a secretary or a vice president. You'd go pick up that envelope from personnel and it would have the directions to the cottage and the keys inside, along with an extra week's pay. It wasn't just Ed's vision that was revolutionary. It was the way he cared about the people who worked for him. Of course all that ended when the money guys took over."

"The money guys?" Kate raised an eyebrow.

"Yeah, the money guys, Kate. The senior management team who took over the company when Ed retired. They weren't people-focused like Ed. They were the money guys."

"Ah," Kate replied. "I understand. I must say I never dreamed I'd personally know so many millionaires. Twenty-seven Easton executives woke up one morning last fall as newly minted millionaires, simply as a result of the merger." She shook her head, "Overnight, just like *that*," Kate snapped her fingers, "their fortunes were made."

"So tell me Kate," Fred asked. "What made those twenty-seven people so special? What made them more deserving than you or me?"

"Good question, Fred. Kismet, perhaps? I don't think we'll ever know."

The eBay Chronicles

Pratt-Miles' director of purchasing was an energetic and brazen young man named Blair Christie. After joining the company, he quickly gained notoriety among senior management. He proposed using eBay to efficiently dispose of the company's outdated office equipment and furnishings while generating modest cash flow. The division vice president gave Blair a month to demonstrate the cost-benefit of using eBay at the corporate level. Three weeks later Blair sent the VP a report reflecting a tidy profit on the disposition of thousands of dollars worth of used company property that had been sitting in a rented storage facility. From that day on, Blair's title might as well have been eBay Wizard.

For Blair Christie, the Easton/Pratt-Miles merger was the corporate equivalent of getting the key to a rich and discriminating grandma's attic. Following the close of the sale, as the audit reports from the field rolled in one after another, Blair's email inbox filled up with bits of information from different department heads about possible assets to be sold.

There was the usual long list of excess computers and related office machine paraphernalia, furniture, and company cars. Also, an entire set of skybox tickets for the local NFL games where the waiting list for season ticket holders was often decades long.

But the fun stuff was comprised of The Easton Company's unique art trove. All these pieces were one-of-a-kind art and artifacts that The Easton Company had displayed throughout the headquarters building during its history. This was the stuff that made Blair Christie salivate as he anticipated watching the eBay bidding. Included in this haul and stored in a warehouse in the Washington suburbs were some museum-worthy 1960s pop artwork, a wooden carousel horse from the Chicago Worlds Fair, an antique pig weathervane rescued in the '70s from a colonial building in Boston slated for demolition, and a Hepworth sculpture.

The real find – the equivalent of an Antiques Road Show jackpot with provenance – had been sent over from a law clerk in the legal division. It was an Iron Mountain box labeled "HRH docs/gloves/goggles" with an accompanying note from the clerk that read simply, "What do you make of this? For real?"

When Blair opened the box, what he saw first was old packing material. But buried deep in the folds was a pair of very worn brown leather gloves that appeared to be quite old. The condition of the leather reminded him of his grandfather's WWII bomber jacket. Underneath the gloves was a pair of goggles that looked as old as the gloves. They had dark green glass with leather straps and an antique fastening clasp. Tucked into one side of the box was an aged folder containing three short documents.

The first paper appeared to be an original, typed on yellowing onionskin typewriter paper. It was a note of appreciation for the recipient's "heroic actions in saving my life. In addition to the mementos I left with you that day, please accept as my gratitude my promise to pay you and your family $150 a month for the rest of your lives." The note was signed in blue fountain pen ink: HRH.

The next document was three pages long and also typewritten. It explained that the aviation goggles and the gloves had originally belonged to Howard Hughes. He had given them as a token of appreciation to a young farmer in whose field Hughes had crash-landed a plane decades before. The farmer had seen the plane go down and driven his tractor to the site, helping Hughes out of the wreckage, allegedly saving Hughes' life. When the farmer died, his wife sent the goggles and gloves back to Hughes with a letter thanking him for his generosity and hopeful that the monthly payments would continue. The document stated that upon receiving the wife's note, Hughes instructed his attorneys to draw up a promissory agreement. The agreement assured the payments would continue for the lifetime of the farmer's wife and the lifetimes of their three children.

The last document in the folder was an executed copy of the notarized promissory agreement signed by Howard Hughes. On the final page of the agreement was a handwritten notation, "Easton post-acquisition obligation. December 1989."

Blair Christie held the goggles and the gloves in his hands and felt his fingers and toes tingle. He'd seen a lot of good stuff in his days, but this was definitely a defining moment. He carefully placed the items back in the box and called the senior Pratt-Miles accountant in charge of cataloging all the periodic cash obligations they had taken over from Easton post-merger. He asked her to look for payments to any of the names shown in the promissory agreement and call him back as soon as possible. Thirty minutes later his phone rang.

"OK. This is weird. Apparently there are three annuity-type payments of fifty dollars each going out monthly to the last three names you gave me. Unlike the other monthly payments we inherited, these aren't marked retiree or employee. In fact, there's no notation explaining what they are. Nothing showing up for the first woman's name, though. What's this all about?" the accountant asked.

"I'll send you a copy of the documentation for the payments that I just found. Once you've read it, come see me and I'll give you the rest of the story," Blair offered. "Gotta go."

Two more hours of phone calls and Blair had most of the story nailed down. The $150 monthly annuity was still being divided among and paid to the farmer's three surviving children, now in their sixties. Both the physical assets and the liabilities had passed to The Easton Company after it acquired a small office park in Las Vegas that included a hangar, transportation offices and several hundred acres of land that belonged to the Hughes heirs.

For Blair Christie, the find of a lifetime was in his possession. He imagined himself much older, telling his future children and grandchildren the Howard Hughes story. No doubt the keepsakes would bring a tidy sum to the company; which would, of course, help boost what was sure to be a very fat year-end bonus for the Pratt-Miles eBay Wizard.

Bottle and the Damage Done

Tim Ferris, Easton's short-term director of auditing, wasn't the first employee let go after the merger, but he might have been the employee who took it hardest.

Pratt-Miles eliminated Tim's job one month after the merger closed and just days before Christmas. The layoff took place less than a year after Easton lured him away from his prior employer, another Fortune 500 company. In his current circumstances, the job that Tim abandoned so readily for Easton now seemed more wonderful and promising than he ever imagined while he was actually in it.

With less than a year of service at The Easton Company, Tim's severance package was the equivalent of a Happy Meal compared to the payouts his longer-term peers at Easton were receiving. All the promises that were made when he took the Easton job just didn't have time to materialize. And when his job was eliminated, the executives who had made those promises were no longer present. It seemed more than unfair to Tim. He felt royally screwed.

By mid-January, Tim had filed a lawsuit against both Easton and Pratt-Miles claiming breach of contract and other allegations piled on by his attorney. Tim sued for a severance package he would have received if he had worked at Easton for ten years; not just eleven months. If the company had not been acquired, Tim argued, he would have stayed for at least a decade. Although it sounded a bit unorthodox, the overall legal argument seemed to make sense. At least that's what his attorney kept telling him. After five months, however, Pratt-Miles offered and Tim – on advice of counsel – accepted a meager $3,000 settlement, most of which went for legal fees.

Tim was angry. His general good mood and easy disposition had vanished in the six months after the merger closed. He woke up angry and went to bed angry. No one wanted to be near him. His anger made it difficult for him to interview for new jobs, even though he was well qualified.

Being home for months with the twins and his wife was making Tim edgy. He was definitely getting on his wife's nerves. He talked constantly about how he had been cheated. She wanted him to get over it and move on. He was embittered, resentful and having trouble letting go.

When Tim's unemployment benefits ran out, his wife noticed her husband more frequently standing at the kitchen sink staring out the window with a whiskey glass in his hand. When he started pouring his first drink before noon, she calmly suggested he needed help.

Hell, he knew he needed help. What did she think the past six months were all about? But clearly the kind of help she was suggesting was not the kind of help Tim had in mind.

A year later, sitting in a group counseling session in the rehab center, Tim knew exactly when his fate had changed and when he started drinking seriously. He told the group it started long before the lawsuit and before the constant anger had settled in. It started before all the unsuccessful job interviews and the split with his wife and his loss of joint custody of his children. He could trace it all back to that morning when he got the flat tire and the call about the sale of The Easton Company. After sopping up his sweat with a disposable diaper and hobbling home in his wife's car on the donut spare, he walked into the house at 10 a.m. and poured himself a large tumbler of whiskey. A song was playing on the radio in the kitchen – he never did figure out the name of the song or the group. But as he sat there in a sweaty Armani suit, the lyrics seemed written for him in that moment in time:

I've been cheated, I've been lied to,
I've been misunderstood and told I'm no good.

"Those lyrics have been spinning through my head for months," Tim told his group. "Now what I want most is to turn back the clock. I have given this a lot of thought. At first I wanted to turn the clock back to that morning on the side of the road, thinking if I had another chance, I wouldn't start drinking. But on further reflection…"

"And many more hours of therapy," one of the group members inserted.

Tim only half grinned, "On further reflection and *additional therapy*, I am now certain I want to turn the clock back to before I left my prior job." Tim went on to describe his wonderful position with the international Fortune 500 firm that provided him a lucrative lifestyle and lots of exciting travel. "I would have made senior vice president by now, no question," Tim concluded. "And the travel would have taken me away from home enough to keep my marriage intact and provide some distance from the demands of toddler twin boys." Tim leaned back in his chair and folded his arms, indicating he was done.

The group counselor shook his head. "Tim, unfortunately the time machine has yet to be invented. Instead of looking back, you should look to the future to sort out your life problems and rectify your current situation."

Not likely, Tim thought to himself as the group discussion passed to the next participant. Tim's wife had recently filed for divorce. Unbeknownst to her, the money required for him to settle his debts was long gone. He had blown through his severance payments and the little bit of savings that remained after the twins were born. He even spent all his retirement money, including his 401(k) assets and pension plan distribution, which required forging his wife's signature on the documents. No, Tim thought. Looking forward was definitely not the answer.

As the group discussion droned on, Tim began to daydream about each brand of whiskey he had ever tasted, in alphabetical order.

Tales of the Sofa – Down-Streamed

The Easton yellow sofa sat on the loading dock at the rear entrance of the former headquarters building. Unfortunately, the sofa's last caretakers were located on the lower level of the building where damage from the storms had caused the roof to leak and ceilings to cave in. In the clean up, the sofa was discovered soaked with water and covered by crumbling ceiling tiles and fallen insulation. Unpleasant brown water stains obscured its once light yellow leather. The sofa's fill had shifted to one side giving it a lopsided look, yet The Easton Company logo was still visible.

It sat for weeks just inside the loading dock door next to the huge dehumidifiers used to dry out the building. But the sofa remained soggy. After someone tracked the awful smell on the lower level to the moldy sofa, the thing was finally banished outside onto the loading dock to await the monthly bulk rubbish pick up.

More than fifteen months had passed since Jim Fisher first found the sofa abandoned in Jeffrey Elkins' former office. It had traveled from the dark corner of a deserted executive suite through a series of users all over the building. Each person had prized the sofa for a different reason.

The sofa on the loading dock looked forlorn and forgotten, but even there it wasn't lonely. Don "don't call me Miami Vice" Johnson was an old homeless guy who hung out near lakeside and slept in the woods until the weather turned too cold. He discovered the yellow sofa soon after its relocation to the loading dock. Although damp and smelly, it was the softest thing the old man had slept on in a long time. Don Johnson had been homeless long enough to know that a human nose exposed to bad smells would eventually tune them out, unless it was the smell of sickness or something long dead. With his equally odorous sleeping bag rolled out on top of the lopsided mass of sagging leather, he found he could get his old bones quite comfortable. Plus, in the event of rain, the loading dock was partially under cover.

The night Mr. Johnson first discovered the sofa, it sat facing the parking lot. Standing on one arm of the sofa under cover of darkness, he was able to reach up and unscrew the outdoor overhead spotlight that lit most of the loading dock. Then he proceeded to maneuver the sofa bit by bit until it faced the building. Jim Fisher would have appreciated the way old Mr. Johnson carefully worked first one end of the sofa and then the other to position it where he wanted it. Anyone passing by would see the back of the sofa but not the person sleeping on it. If it weighed 150 pounds the night Jim relocated it to his office, it now weighed twice that much, water soaked as it was.

Don Johnson had his routines. Each evening when the last cars pulled away from the building and most of the joggers had finished their circuits, he would wander up to the loading dock and take a look around. When the coast was clear he shifted his old army surplus backpack off his shoulder and hefted it up onto the concrete dock. Following another scan of the area, he pulled his tired old self up onto the ledge of the dock and sat with his feet dangling off the side for a handful of minutes. Sometimes the local security guards made rounds at dusk so he resisted getting too comfortable until they passed by. Once his sleeping bag was in place he would open his pack and extract a pint of Old Crow or some Wild Irish Rose, depending on his fiscal situation. Following his first swig, he settled onto the sofa and reached into his pack again. The two items he brought out next had traveled with him for the past seven years. After placing the pair of objects carefully on the loading dock floor in front of the sofa, he took another pull on the bottle and then the conversation began.

For the better part of two weeks Don Johnson repeated his nightly routine undetected and was long gone before the first cars pulled into the lot in the morning.

One evening, inside the building, young and eager Alex Higgins was working late. Hired post-merger as a junior accountant, he had volunteered to stay all night if necessary to unravel a tricky accounting issue for his boss at Pratt-Miles headquarters in Denver. Alex liked working after everyone else had gone home. It gave him an opportunity to explore the interesting spaces within the old Easton headquarters building. At night, he could relocate to different offices and enjoy a new view each time.

On this particular evening, Alex decided to move with his laptop, cell phone and his project files to an empty office facing the lake. Within the building's boxy design, this particular office stuck out from the main portion of the building with windows facing three directions. Alex observed that the expansive view of trees, lake and sky was fantastic as long as you didn't look down. Looking down and to the left provided a side view of the loading dock and the adjacent dumpsters.

Sometime around 9 p.m., after returning from a trip to the men's room, Alex heard a distinctive voice coming from outside. It was a low tenor voice with a slight southern texture to it. It sounded like half of a conversation. Alex walked to the windows and looked down toward the dumpsters trying to locate the source of the voice. It was very dark at the back of the building, but a full moon helped Alex spot an old man sitting on a sofa on the loading dock. The man was definitely having a conversation with someone, apparently to his left, although Alex couldn't actually see anyone. The talk continued and Alex looked hard out the window in an attempt to locate the other person. But he couldn't see anyone there. So Alex listened harder to hear what the old man was saying:

"Don't you think so? Yep, that's my thoughts 'xactly. I knew it all the time. He never fooled me once, darlin'," and then the old man laughed. It wasn't the laugh of a crazy man, Alex thought. It was the laugh of someone recalling a funny story, a good joke, an old friend who could make him chuckle.

Feeling as though he was eavesdropping, Alex took a step back from the windows, suddenly concerned about being detected by the old man. He didn't want to interrupt. With just the desk lamp on in the office, he moved into the shadows but could still see the loading dock. He wanted to hear and see more.

"We sure had some good times with him tho' didn't we, darlin'," the man said to the empty space next to him on the sofa. Watching the old guy take a drink from a bottle in his hand, Alex spotted something red and shiny in a pool of moonlight on the floor of the loading dock in front of the sofa. It took a minute for Alex to realize what he was seeing. Then, like an Escher drawing, the objects came into focus: a pair of bright red stiletto high heels. The shoes looked quite worn but in the moonlight appeared to be recently polished. Or possibly they were patent leather, Alex thought. The shoes were parked neatly, toes pointed out, next to the talker's feet.

"Yes um. Those were mighty fine times we used to have." Hearing that sentence, Alex realized the old man's conversation was with an imaginary person in those red shoes.

The voice started up again, but more slurred for the alcohol. Alex shook his head and retreated to the desk, feeling the need to accomplish some work before going home. He tried to focus on the contents of a file, but instead found himself concentrating on what the man under the window was saying. "So what's it gonna be for dinner tonight, darlin'? Chicken you say? You do like your chicken don't you now…"

Alex closed the file he'd been holding and decided to call it a night. There was little chance of getting any more work done with his head full of the conversation from the loading dock sofa. Driving home, he began wondering exactly who the old guy was talking to. A past girlfriend? His deceased wife?

Possibly his mother? Or maybe a sister? Whoever she was, Alex was fairly certain the invisible person had once been flesh and bone. But why the shoes? Did he take them along when he went for chicken? Did they ever go dancing? Where did he put the shoes while he slept? It was those red shoes, not the stubborn accounting question, which kept Alex awake most of the night.

The next morning when Alex arrived at work, he desperately wanted to tell someone – anyone – about what he'd seen and heard on the loading dock the night before. By the light of day, however, the experience seemed more dreamlike than real. After pouring a black coffee in the office kitchenette, he decided to take another look at the loading dock. Walking to the empty office where he had been the previous evening, Alex wondered if the old man or the red shoes might still be there by the sofa. As he entered the office he heard the sound of a large truck accelerating outside. Alex walked quickly to the window, hoping to catch sight of some remnant from the night before. To his surprise, the loading dock was empty. Even the sofa had disappeared. Again the truck engine roared and he looked across the parking lot just in time to see a city refuse truck pull away around the corner with one end of the old yellow sofa protruding from the back.

Alex shook his head and walked away. It was clear where the sofa was headed, but he tried hard not to dwell on the whereabouts of the homeless drunk and the red shoes.

Easton Transportation – Final Flight

Jake Martin sat at an empty desk he had dragged out into the hangar bay from the office. It was the lone piece of furniture remaining in the building. All outstanding bills for Easton Transportation were paid months ago. At the request of Pratt-Miles management, he recently packed up the subsidiary's complete onsite files and shipped them to Denver. Jake held on to his own personal flight records, but he wasn't sure why.

A call had just come in on his Blackberry with news that today's potential buyer for the hangar was experiencing flight delays and running very late. However, they would definitely be there as soon as possible. So he was waiting.

To kill time he decided to review some of those flight records, but it only reminded him how long it had been since he'd done any serious flying. He handled the papers just to keep his hands busy while he permitted himself some aviation daydreams.

Certainly sometime soon the hangar would sell and he'd start looking for a new corporate gig. Possibly something overseas this time…maybe on the Mediterranean. Effortlessly, Jake's hands moved over the papers in front of him, reflecting his deepest obsession.

If Jeffrey Elkins had flipped open his laptop at that very moment and logged on to the hangar's ceiling security webcam, he would have seen a curious sight: an exquisitely folded white paper airplane making a precise arc across the hangar, gracefully pirouetting and landing atop a large squadron of identical aircraft.

Postscript – Some Last Thoughts About Corporations as Employers

Corporations exist to serve their shareholders. The law actually requires corporations to put the financial interests of their shareholders – in the form of profits – above all else, even to the exclusion of the corporation's stakeholders, such as the community and its employees.

– The Corporation
2004 Documentary Film
Directed by Mark Achbar, Jennifer Abbott, and Joel Bakan

And therein sat the crux of the problem. The Easton Company had been founded by a man dedicated to the common good, the community, and the company's employees. Later, he founded a nonprofit he nicknamed the Robin Hood Foundation and devoted his retirement years to humanely housing the poor in the nation's inner cities. Along the way, he received the Presidential Medal of Freedom, changed the face of decaying urban landscapes, and stood alone as a selfless CEO in a business world that was becoming greedy.

In his lifetime, Ed Easton employed thousands of people who came to believe as he did – that the community was all-important, and that every employee mattered. Ed Easton believed in that dream and lived it. When "the money guys" sold out seven years after Easton's death, many of his disciples were still employed at the company and hundreds of retirees were among the disbelievers about the merger events that unfolded. Shock and disgust were among the emotions of these individuals who called themselves Ed's Pioneers. The idea that the money guys would break the social contract with the company's retirees, employees and the community was unfathomable.

Post-Mortem

Steven Pearlstein in the *Washington Post* insightfully wrote:

"After a major merger, sometime down the road, the merged companies confront a truth everyone knows but nobody seems to remember in the adrenaline rush of announcing a major deal: Mergers and acquisitions are always hard, usually overpriced, rarely as imperative as portrayed – and they almost never work out as planned."

The terms of the merger in this story called for Easton stockholders to get a thirty-three percent premium on their shares. The news caused Easton shares to advance to more than $60 by market close on the day after the deal was announced. On that same day Pratt-Miles' shares slipped to close at $30 – less than half the offer price per share on the company they were buying.

At the time, Pratt-Miles executives said the premium they paid was justified because of the potential for higher revenue and lower overhead. Hailing Easton's collection of properties as well-managed, Pratt-Miles' CEO said the deal positioned his company to be "the industry leader in all aspects of our business."

What went largely unrecognized at the time of the merger was that in purchasing Easton, Pratt-Miles assumed nearly $6 billion in Easton debt as part of the deal. Most of that debt was scheduled to come due in less than five years. At the time of the merger, Easton's senior financial executives had shared with fellow employees behind closed doors, "There is no way Pratt-Miles will ever be able to successfully pay off that debt."

Pratt-Miles stock never traded as high as the premium price paid for The Easton Company, although it did at one point reach $51 a share. Then, just twelve months later, Pratt-Miles entered a financial perfect storm. In the midst of an unprecedented international economic downturn, the company faced an impending debt payoff deadline for nearly a billion dollars. With no long-term financing available Pratt-Miles found itself on the brink of bankruptcy, with its stock trading as low as twenty-five cents a share.

These issues and problems prompted Pratt-Miles to state in a Securities and Exchange Commission filing that there were "...substantial doubts as to our ability to continue as an ongoing concern." Then the company proceeded to report a quarterly loss of more than $15 million. Within a month the company suspended its dividend and halted plans for any new ventures. Pratt-Miles unsuccessfully attempted to sell off some of its prime properties in order to pay a $900 million mortgage that was coming due with no lenders willing to provide that amount of refinancing. During the same period the CEO and CFO both stepped down from their positions. Four years, five months and two days after completing its merger with The Easton Company, Pratt-Miles declared bankruptcy in the biggest real estate failure in U.S. history.

Pratt-Miles was clearly the python that swallowed the pig...and choked. Reflective of its times, Pratt-Miles became the poster child of mergers and acquisitions that didn't work out.

Author's Note

THE NOVEL IS A WAY OF SPEAKING THE TRUTH THAT FACTS FAIL TO UNCOVER.

As is always the case in fiction writing, I have been inspired by people I have known, events I have witnessed, and conversations that did in fact occur, stories I've been told and information I have read. Still and all, this book exists solely as an imaginary tale set in very real times.

Readers familiar with the merger and acquisition activity in the Philadelphia to Richmond corridor during the early years of the twenty-first century are reminded that *Pink Slips and Parting Gifts* is a work of fiction. Events, people, places, statistics, words and deeds have all passed through the doors of my mind's eye before entering the text of this novel.

The Easton Company, Pratt-Miles, their employees, and other characters in this book as I've described them are the stuff of make-believe and imagination. All locations and historical references, corporate lore and news items are used fictionally. Sometimes names have been changed, sometimes not.

Though descriptions and references may hold some kernel of fact or familiarity to certain individuals, all have been fictionalized – even if not entirely beyond recognition, then definitely into the world of fable, make-believe, and legend.

About the Author

Deb Hosey White is an executive management consultant with more than thirty years experience working for Fortune 1000 companies. She is the co-author of *Beyond Downton Abbey* — a guide to 25 great houses in Britain, and *Let's Take the Kids to London* — a family travel guidebook. Both books are written with David Stewart White, her best friend and travel companion.

Also by the author

Let's Take the Kids to London
by David Stewart White
and Deb Hosey White

Beyond Downton Abbey
by Deb Hosey White
and David Stewart White

Acknowledgments

Thanks to my family and fine friends who encouraged this project to conclusion. Special thanks to my rough draft readers and editors, and to my book group buddies in Maryland.

To my husband, David, for his persistent critique and constant support, I tender my deepest gratitude.

Finally, a nod to my original Monopoly partners, Tommy and Casey, who never dreamed the scrawny little blonde who never won and always cried would grow up to be a benefits nerd and business guru. Thanks for letting me play.